KALKHUNTA: A LIVING ANCESTRAL HERITAGE

A Panorama of Bastar

KALKHUNTA: A LIVING ANCESTRAL HERITAGE

A Panorama of Bastar

K. M. Sinha Roy

Co-author

Rajesh Roshan

Vijay Kumar

AAYU

AAYU PUBLICATIONS

New Delhi-110086

Cataloging in Publication Data--DK
Courtesy: D.K. Agencies (P) Ltd. <docinfo@dkagencies.com>

Sinha Roy, K. M., author.
Kalkhunta : a living ancestral heritage : a panorama of baster / K.M. Sinha Roy, Rajesh Roshan, Vijay Kumar. -- First edition.
pages cm
Includes bibliographical references.
ISBN 9789391685256

1. Maria (Indic people)--India--Bastar--Rites and ceremonies. 2. Muria (Indic people)--India--Bastar--Rites and ceremonies. 3. Ancestor worship--India--Bastar. 4. Burial--India--Bastar. 5. Megalithic monuments--India--Bastar. 6. Bastar (India)--Antiquities. I. Roshan, Rajesh (Research officer of social studies), author. II. Kumar, Vijay (Research associate (cultural)), author. III. Title.

LCC DS432.M267S56 2022 | DDC 305.800954137 23

Published by:

AAYU PUBLICATIONS
D-134, Agar Nagar, Prem Nagar-III
New Delhi-110086
Tel: 09910728725, 09654504227
Email: aayupublication@gmail.com
www.aayupublications.com

Kalkhunta: A living ancestral Heritage a Panorama of Bastar

First Edition 2023

ISBN: 978-93-91685-25-6

PRINTED IN INDIA

Printed at Unitech Graphic Point, Delhi

Dedicate to

Late Professor **Vinay Kumar Srivastava**

Former Director Anthropological Survey of India For his guidance and suggestion for final shape of this volume

FOREWORD

Indian culture comprises the cultural heritages of several ethnic groups. Each and every culture is unique in many respects.

Amidst such uniqueness one may find existence of similarities in some elements of cultural traditions among the diverse populations distributed in different ecological settings across the length and breadth of the country.

A few tribes and folk people living in relatively secluded geographical regions could continue with their unique cultures in the ever-increasing impact of advanced scientific knowledge and technology of their neighbouring cultures.

Megalithic culture of Iron Age, seen in practice among some ethnic groups in contemporary India, is a glaring example of such continuation of traditions.

Megaliths in India drew academic attention of the Archaeologists when J. Babington reported burial monuments of *Bangla Motta Paramba* at Malabar of Kerala in 1823. Initial approach of the archaeologists was to know the antiquity of the megaliths. In later period their focus shifted towards understanding cultural heritage of the people.

To the anthropologists megaliths became handy in analyzing elements of social organization of the communities pursuing the custom of erecting monolithic memorial pillars. Their primary interest centered on understanding beliefs of the tribes associated with the memorial pillars, functions of the maternal and paternal kin members, clans, and phratries in bringing all the members together, that ultimately help regenerating and consolidating their social bond and perpetuation of social and religious customs.

Tradition of erecting megalithic pillars by the Gonds and some Naga and the Khasi people of the Central and Northeast India respectively, have been reported as a part of ethnographic works of Verrier Elwin (Funerary Customs in Bastar State, *Man in India*, 1945) and Von Furrer Haimendorf (The problem of Megalithic Culture of Middle India, *Man in India,*1945).

Elwin's anthropological perspectives underline reasons of persistence of megalithic cultural practices that are apparent in the beliefs of the Gonds. They believe that a soul of the ancestor remains within these pillars and protect their clans. Such beliefs of sepulchral nature pave the ways in continuation of cultural practices through generations. These observations are suggestive of having direct and intimate relation of the memorial pillars with the life and cultures of the Gond tribes of Bastar. Haimendorf pointed out similarities in customs and rituals of the tribes living faraway from each other in two different geographical conditions.

As I read the present anthropological work "*Kalkhunta: A Living Ancestral Heritage: A Panorama of Bastar*, authored by K.M. Sinha Roy, Rajesh Roshan and Vijay Kumar, I feel happy to see the quantity and quality of the data they have placed before the readers for examining the cultural processes that push forward continuity of cultural traditions. I am not at all surprised to note that the kin groups from *Akomama* and *Dadabhai* phratries perform the roles in the same ways as Elwin had observed about 75 years back, keeping their basic cultural norms and practices least effected. In fact, this is an inherent phenomenon of the belief system concerning survival and wellbeing of community and therefore, the traditions survive.

These three authors, as members of the Anthropological Survey of India's office at Jagdalpur, had ample scope to be in regular touch with the Gonds of Bastar for few years. Their insights reflected in the 'thick description' of the book remind the readers that the creative excellence of these tribes embedded with sentiment in these 'tangible cultural heritage' are deep rooted in their culture. These are also value loaded and are of outstanding aesthetic importance and equally significant for the culture of the community.

Pictorial views of the memorial pillars with explanatory notes are of great significance in terms of disseminating anthropological knowledge to all categories of readers.

At the end of this elaborate account of megalithic culture in contemporary Bastar, the authors have placed a note of caution that "adequate measures must be developed to safeguard this heritage". Safeguarding such cultural heritage is a difficult proposition in the rapidly changing surroundings, though various institutions of the Government of India and also of the State, through their museums and archives have been extending necessary supports in this direction. However, without the active involvement of the members of these tribes it would not be easy to achieve the desired goal.

Lovers of tribal heritage may play a meaningful role in convincing these tribes that their age-old cultural practices have great significance towards shaping the Great Indian culture unique in all respects.

In this context this comprehensive account of the megalithic cultural heritage authored by three anthropologists would be an inspiring resource.

Authors of this book deserve special appreciation from the scholars interested in looking at uniqueness of cultural heritages of people of India, in general and tribes of India, in particular.

Jayanta Sarkar
Former Director-in-Charge,
Anthropological Survey of India,
Government of India

PREFACE

Bastar is a homeland of multiethnic unique culture. Hence, the indigenous tribes living here since ages long and have maintained their distinct identity. Ancestor reverence is not the same as regards worshipping of deities. Throughout the globe, some of the communities' ancestors are seen as being able to intercede on behalf of the living, often as messengers between humans and gods. In India, when a person dies, the family observes mourning as customary period, called 'Sraddha' derived from a Sanskrit sentence "Shraddhayat diote" means what is offered with deep respect in memory of the deceased. After one year or six months, they observe the ritual of 'Tarpan' to the deceased. Beside, these some other necessary rituals known as funerary monuments (Memorial Pillars) as found in some communities in India. The act is a way to respect, honour and look after ancestors in their after lives as well as seek their guidance for their living descendants.

In the context of Bastar, in the Gonds and other subgroups, when a person dies the family observes seven to thirteen days mourning period known as '*Kriya Karma*' and '*Sutak*' etc. (as per customs). After mourning for six months to one year, the people observe different types of ancestral ceremonies as per customary traditions. But in case of the indigenous tribes like the Bison Horn Maria, the Muria, and the Raj Gond they generally perform "*Math Munda*" or "*Kalkhunta*" or "*Gata Khunta*" ceremony. The ceremony is generally held after 10 – 15 years or even 25 years. Before, the ceremony the head of the family calls a meeting within clan group or relatives. On the day all the clan people and relatives fix the day of the ceremony and announcement is made and the present clan people as well as relatives declare their individual support in cash or kind according to their capacity to make the ceremony successful. The types of memorial pillars raised and erected in Bastar region are mainly *uraskal* (stone memorials), *danyakal*, wooden pillar, painted Memorials, *maths* (Cenotaph).

The objective of these memorials is survival; not only perpetuation of the clan, but also to present a brief clan detail about their forefathers or ancestors through this pillar to their future generation's wellbeing. The *uraskal*, *danyakal*, and *kalkhunta* represent the final step, and they do not merely indicate the desire to honour the dead, but they also indicate the desire to promote the spiritual union with the ancestors. Each stone, wooden pillar, math, therefore adds to the collective strength of the group as a whole and ultimately of the clan in its link with earth and the spirits of the departed.

ACKNOWLEDGEMENT

The outcome of the book reflected series of ancestral erection of memorial pillar panorama scattered in the Bastar region. The memorial pillar has bearing with Historical, Archaeological and Religious heritage values of the Gond communities. We hope all the research scholars will know about the Neolithic and Megalithic memorial culture which still continues among the Gonds of Bastar.

Sincere thanks to some of our colleagues and research scholars of Anthropological survey of India. Sub-regional centre, Jagdalpur, who obliged us with their gracious presence during the fieldwork. We sincerely thank Shri Palash Jalani, Shri, B.Ramkumar, Smt. Beena Vishwakarma for their assistance in report writing. We are also indebted to Shri Abhijit Shrivastava and Shri Shukuram Kashyap, Shri, Narendra Kumar Bhaghel, for their day-to-day involvement during fieldwork.

We also acknowledge with sincere regards Prof. Basant Lal Jha, eminent scholar of Bastar, for his generous help and cooperation.

We express our thankfulness to Sukma, Dantewada, Bijapur and Abujmarh district Administration, Panchayats and their staff for providing us important information and extending all logistic support during the course of the fieldwork.

Last but not the least; we are indebted to fieldwork village people, who helped us in a number of ways in the face of the Naxalite hazard.

Authors

CONTENTS

1

CHAPTER

INTRODUCTION

Everyone wonders what makes our lives so eventful, it is death. That is so because we know that humans are mortal and everyone within his or her life has a tremendous urge to mark ourselves by work, art, and every means in the world. As Malinowski had reported 'The supreme and final crisis of life is Death' (1948). The significance of the term creates problems at individual level; or the society as a whole. A dead person is believed to disturb or creates problem in individual's social relations, family, economic activities, and emotional exchange. Besides, the death interacts and creates stress which pervades the entire social structure in social relationships.

The social importance of the deceased will vary from community to community. The loss of any member from the group will have repercussions in a much wider circle than that composed of kin's. The empirical records show that, the Masai, the plain Indian, and the Eskimo; death loses its sting when it is not conceived of as complete end of the self.) This cultural potential, the possibility of partially alleviating individual fears regarding death through the implicit belief in an afterlife stands as another virtually universal feature of human existence.

Belief in the existence of superhuman of supernatural powers is almost universal. Experiences of certain day-of-day sudden happenings, of disease, death and the unexplainable, have led tribal people into believing in other the material visible word i.e., in the invisible spirit-world or supernatural power. They have established a kind of close relationship between themselves and this power by adjusting themselves to it in two ways, first by controlling or overpowering the spirit by enchanting or practicing some techniques and canalizing the power, for good or bad, and secondly, by offering *puja* or worship to propitiate the superhuman power for acquisition of the thing or object desired. We call the former magic and the letter religion. In the tribal's magic is actually as integral part of their religion and magical practices may be included as a method of propitiation. Lowie (1950; 176) also includes all forms of super naturalism including magic in religion.

The activities of ancestors are quite evident for the tribal's and ancestor worship finds an important place in their religious beliefs. They recognize that man's power is restricted and that he has access to limited areas, but through ancestor worship, he acquires powers of a far-reaching and compulsive kind. They believe in the existence of ancestors and their interest and intervention in the worldly affairs, they are at work in their real life. Dube (1970) and Vidyarthi (1963; 144) consider ancestor worship an important aspect of the tribal religion. Since the tribal's firmly believe in the idea that spirits of the dead ancestors have power to decide their destiny, they are very cautious in performing the rites and observe all the ceremonies carefully. The newly dead person is believed to have joined the earlier dead ancestors. The spirits of ancestors are called and worshipped, (i) annually, (ii) occasionally or (iii) when one is economically able to perform it. The tribal's believe that unless the spirit of the newly dead ancestor is worshipped it continues to exists, and appears in dreams. It always harasses its relatives to expedite the preparation for worship, mortuary sacrifice and feast.

Regarding survival of the human spirit after death, Frazer wrote "it seems probable that the great majority of our species will continue to acquiesce in a belief so flattering to human vanity and so comforting to human sorrow (1890)". It is believed that, in an after world an individual is more or less in intimate contact with the departed members of his own group or with the spirits of all departed human beings. Besides, in many groups, spirits may be partially evil or dangerous to the lives of the living. When spirit is very close to its own kin group the kin group feels that the spirit requires propitiation by the rest of the kin group. Thus ancestor worship prevails.

The people remember their ancestors from kinship system to kinship system. For example, some Asian and African people may remember ancestors up to twenty ascending generations. In the Chinese ancestral hall, among the Merina of Madagascar or many aboriginal Australians it has been observed that, men and women may be remembered equally. In patrilineal system ancestors in the male line are remembered and it is reverse in matrilineal system. Here, in Bastar the patrilineal society gives importance to concept clan and descent plays a vital role.

Ancestor worship is a phrase used to denote religious practices concerned with the belief that dead forebears can in some way influence the living. In Tallensi of Ghana, Fortes stresses how the worship which a patrilineal descendant should carry out reflects, though in a subtly changed way, the relationship of father and son when living (Fortes 1959). In these systems the ancestors are believed to exercise a moral guardianship over their descendants so that they do not quarrel among themselves. In case of Bastar region, the people of Maria and Muria they observe ancestral worship from generation to generation for their wellbeing as mentioned (Roy, Roshan, and Kumar, -16). The people of Maria and Muria of Bastar region observe ancestral worship by erecting memorial stones carry with the desire to custom, social values and wellbeing for the society. The *kal khunta* is a living cultural symbol of Bastar. It is an ancestral worship panorama of the region which is performed by the people after 20 to 30 years within the clan groups.

While working in Bastar, the study realized this notion that the continuity of soul is not just a concept, but has been in practice throughout this multi-cultural diverse India. From the Sabars of West Bengal, Mundas and Oraons of Odisha to the Nagas of the North-East, there are prolonged after-death rituals performing to worshiping the dead to ensure rebirth and also for blessings from the dead. The Gonds of Bastar region are also no different from the others. They erect megaliths in memory of the dead, thus confirming their belief in the existence of soul after death. They also perform rituals to obtain blessings from the dead as they have a concept that after death, the soul remains around them.

In almost all pre historic societies, Megalithic culture has made an endemic presence which is characterized by monuments made of or containing large stones. The pyramids, the stone hedge or other structures throughout the world were built by a common group of people or civilizations during the Neolithic period. Every tradition and culture has its own significance. The study of megalithic culture in the present context takes us through the death practices of the Gonds of Bastar region, their rituals and their beliefs in relation to the erection of memorial pillars in the memory of their ancestor. Ancestor worship is found in almost all cultures of the world. Ancestor veneration is based on love and respect for the departed soul. We feel grateful to our elders for the good they have done to us. Ancestor worship fosters kinship values, such as filial piety, family loyalty and continuity of the family lineage. The living progeny expresses its love and veneration for its deceased ancestors in many ways. Ancestor worship is also based on the belief that the dead have a continuous existence and have the power to influence the lives of the living, that they bestow their blessings if they are propitiated properly. Among the diverse Indian communities, memorial ceremonies are practised in different ways as per their customary beliefs which is related to the concept of rebirth, sin and salvation in memory of the dead person. It is also performed for the welfare of the individual as well as the community. The memorial tradition is reflected differently among different communities through various symbolic ways such as a wooden effigy, stone carving, math etc.

Ancestor reverence is not the same as the worship of deities. In many parts of India ancestors are seen as beings able to intercede on behalf of the living, often as messengers between humans and gods as spirits who were once human themselves. They are seen as being better able to understand human needs than would a divine being. Ancestors are acknowledged and honoured in India among the people. In India, when a person dies, the family observes a ten or more days as mourning period, called *Sraddha*. In a year and six months, they observe the ritual of Tarpan with the family manges offering to the deceased. Besides these necessary some other rituals known as funerary monuments (Memorial Pillars) are found in some communities in India. The Act is a way for their living descendants to honor their guidance and follow their path.

In the context of Bastar region the Gond and other subgroups, when a person dies the family observes seven to fifteen days mourning period known as *Kriya -Karma, Sutak* etc. as per their customs. After mourning for six months to one year, the people observe different types of ancestral ceremonies as tradition followed by them. But in the case of Bison Horn Maria, Muria and Abhuj Maria they generally do erect memorials to their departed persons in the family. The process of erecting memorials is slightly differing to each other. These are *kal khunta, gata pakhna* and *gata khunta, madia khambha,* etc., which have same objectivity. This ceremony is very expensive, therefore so arranged if the family having sufficient provision in his house. It is decided to make the ceremony with the concurred with their kin members. This ceremony generally is held after 20-25 years or even after 30 years. Different types of memorial pillars are found to be raised and erected in Bastar region these are *uraskal* (upright stone memorials) *danyakal* (horizontal slab supported by boulders), *urasgutta* (wooden pillar/post), Painted Stone Memorials, Math (cenotaph) etc.

The purpose of these memorials is survival and not only perpetuation of the clan but also present a brief clan detail about their ancestors through this pillar to their future generation. *Uraskal, Danyakal, Gata Khunta* and *Kal Khunta* not only represent the last stages of life, but also promote spiritual union with ancestors, in honor of the dead. That is why each stone, wooden pillar, adds to the collective power of the monastic group as a whole and ultimately the clan that is associated with the earth and the spirits of the departed.

Account of earlier study on living megalithic culture

The study of burial practices is one of the most important

sources for archaeologist (Alekshin, 1983) and the analysis of ancient burials is very much useful to reconstruct the burial rites (Grayaznov, 1956, Chapman, 1981) and it also reflects the basic feature of the socio-economic structure of primitive tribe (Ravdonikas 1932, Binford 1971). The living megalithic tradition helps in understanding the history of Iron Age communities. At the same time, it is convenient to know about their traditional socio-religious customs; beliefs etc. form those communities who presently erect megalithic to their departed. In India, these burial practices began to originate from the Mesolithic period (Allchin, 1983) and till the beginning of Neolithic age. According to the study of Gupta (1972a), Leshnik (1974), Sahi (1991) and Ranjan (1994), the burial practices continued and exist in Neolithic and Chalcolithic ages throughout this country.

From pre-Iron age Megalithic cultures are found in India. Nowadays these are also continued in few areas. The Gadbas and Bondos are in Central India (Haimendorff, 1943). The Bondo (Elwin, 1950; Tripathy 1969), the Todas (Breeks, 1873, Wall house, 1874a, 1874b), the Kurumbas (Kapp, 1985, Poyil, 2009, 2013) and the Malarayas (Krishna Iyer, 1939) and the Nagas (Singh, 1985; Hutton, 1922, Binodini Devi, 1993, Sharma, 1997, Jamir 1997-98), the Khasi (Austeen, 1872; Gurdon 1907; Baren 1981, Cecile Mawlong, 1990, Rao, 1991), the Marams (Binodivi, 2004), the Jaintias (Marak, 2012), the North Eastern part of India, can be analysed as a form of living megalithic tradition with in the different tribal communities (Devi, 2013).

There are thousands of memorial stones found everywhere but all are not always connected with burials. Some have sculpted scenes (realistic or symbolic) others have inscriptions. Some memorial stones are worshipped (Singh, 2016).

Sharma (2000) work, on "*The Archaeo-Anthropology of Chhattisgarh*" documents that, megalithic culture is a living tradition of the aborigines of Bastar, Manipur and Jharkhand (Hazaribagh & Singhbhum) etc. The traditions of erecting memorials are still practiced amongst the aborigines in Bastar. The size and shapes of the memorials stones differ from area to area, which is erected in the honour of the departed persons in the family. Author pointed that the megalithic of Bastar region are concentrated on high rock bench areas and available on open hills and have no need to dig them out. Author has excavated twelve different types of Megalithic monuments at Karkhabhat in order to ascertain their sepulchral nature and to find out the difference between them. The evidences obtained from excavation clearly shows that the menhirs and cairn circles are not associated with any sepulchral rite. They are only commemorative in nature.

Postel and Cooper's work, on the "The Bastar Folk Art -Shrine, Figurines and Memorials" (1999) deals with the exclusive and fascinating tradition of constructing memorials among the Muria and Maria Gonds. The upright stone, horizontal slab, carved wooden and stone pillars, painted stones are commemorated for the dead person. These have been compared to similar tradition in South India. The memorials are decorated with intricate designs and vivid pictures narrating the life of deceased.

Gupta (1982) contributes information about megalithic culture in Bastar region and adds that the megalithic traditions are surviving among the tribal folks there even in the present time.

Elwin, in his "Maria Murder and Suicide", (1977) Chapter V, describes, how the tribal beliefs and practices came to be believed by the Hindus and Muslims of the Bastar region. He also documents about the funerary rites of the Maria Gonds and their various stages of life cycle in this region in his prestigious work.

Elwin in his paper "Funerary customs in Bastar State" (1945) produces a very detailed and descriptive account of the funerary rites and eschatological beliefs of the aborigines like Hill Maria, Bison Horn Maria and Jhoria Muria of Bastar. Two kinds of megalithic monuments namely *uraskal* and *danyakal*, were erected in honour of the dead. Small cairn *(marma kal/marman gal)* and wooden posts were also erected as substitutes for lithic monuments. The aborigines considered the dead as a guard, keeping close watch with kith and kin. Since the dead are prone to take offence, suspicious, extremely revengeful and unsympathetic, the living aborigine left no stone unturned to keep them in their place. So that the dead could find some warmth and love and receive the comfort they needed.

Haimendorf, in his paper 'The problem of Megalithic culture of Middle India' (1945) references that the similarity of customs and rituals are found between Indian and North East Indian tribes. The megalithic culture of the South East Asiatic type is found among the Gadabas, Bondos and Bastar Gonds who came from the East with its center of diffusion in Eastern Assam or North Burma or China. It is quite likely that there was an earlier migration of Austro-Asiatic culture. This megalithic culture was already developed before commencement of the migration of Austro-Asiatic races westward into peninsular India.

Study area and people

The formerly Bastar district has constituted in 1948 after the merger of feudatory States comprising the erstwhile feudatory States of Bastar and Kanker including the zamindaris thereof. It is the biggest district of the than

Madhya Pradesh in terms of area. The name of the district seems to be have been derived from it. There are two explanations regarding the etymology of the name Bastar. According to one, the word Bastar is corrupt form of the Hindi word *vastra* meaning cloth and refers to the legend of the gift of a piece of cloth by the tutelary deity to the first chief of State.

The land of Bastar has its own historical identity and bears the evidence of diverse archaeological and cultural influences throughout its history. From the empirical records it has been observed that the region was ruled over by various dynasties at different times and periods even through the 20th century. During different political interventions and impact of globalization and modernization the area got transformed in its geo-physical order, the socio-cultural, economic and religious changes happening in accordance with the contextual situation. On 1st November in the year 2000, Chhattisgarh was declared as a State separated from Madhya Pradesh. The State consists of 27 districts, out of which formerly Bastar district maintains its own identity in the field of territorial identity, cultural, linguistic, economic and political spheres. The geo-physical condition of Bastar region has rich potential strength and also rich bio-cultural diversity. Presently, Bastar district is separated into six another districts. The main features of the Bastar territory is the extensive plateau, mainly covered with Sal (shorea robusta) forest stretching from its northern boundary to some distant south of the Indravati river and mainly inhabited by aboriginal known as Murias. The western part of the Bastar territory is tangled mass of hills, known as the Abujmarh, inhabited by the primitive tribe known as the Marias. The southern portion of the Bastar territory along the Godavari river is low lying, hot and damp.

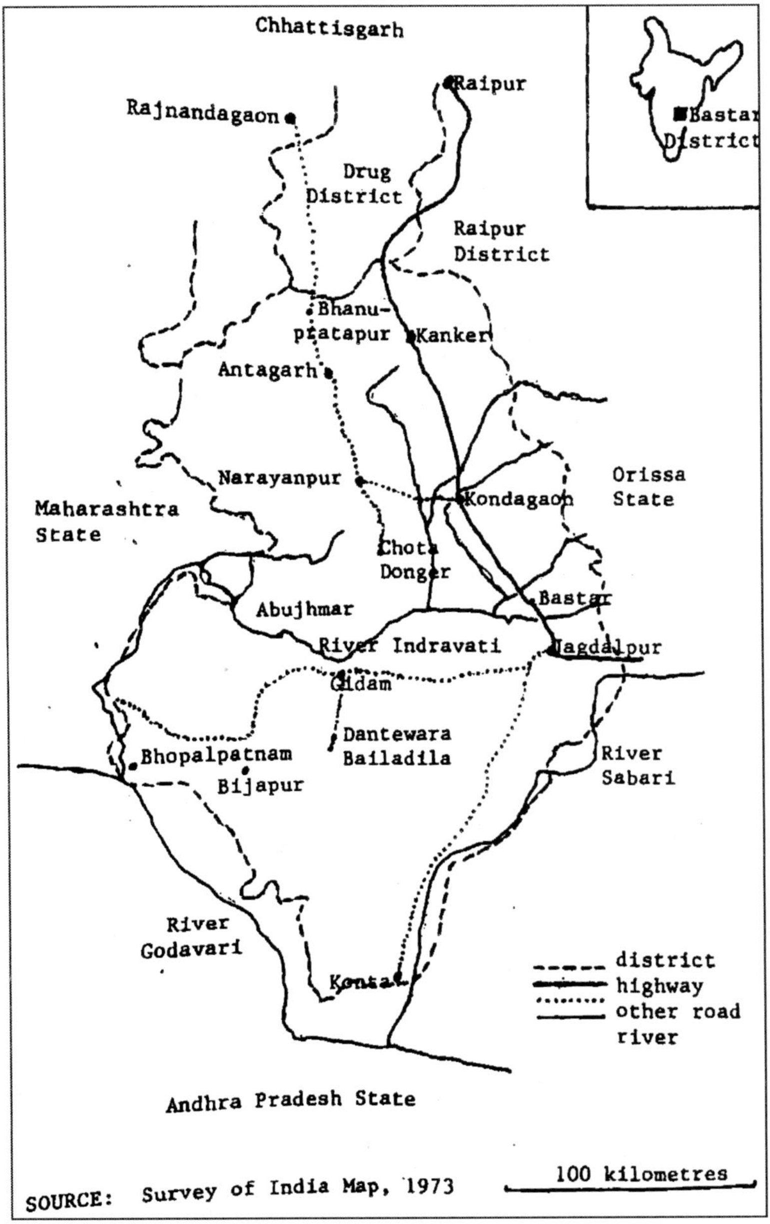

Map 1: Map of Bastar District, Madhya Pradesh

In Bastar different languages are encountered as one by one moving from one area to another though Halbi said to be the lingua-franca langue in the region. The chief languages used in the region are Hindi, Halbi, Chhattisgarhi, Telugu, Dorli, Parja etc., and other various dialects of Gondi. Bhattri a dialect used on the Middle East boarder. The Bhattri is supposed to be a dialect of Oriya and takes its name from the Bhattra tribe of Bastar. This dialect forms a link between Oriya and Halbi. Sir George Grierson holds that Bhattri might equally well be classified along the many form of Halbi as among the dialects of Oriya. (Census of India, 1961)

Huber, 1975 in his thesis entitled *"From Millennia to Millennium, An Anthropological History of Bastar State"* submitted in the University of British Columbia described that Elwin, the missionary turned ethnographer and the man most responsible for bringing Bastar to attention of the rest of India as well as to Anthropology. His description of Bastar resonates with the fondness so characteristic of his explorations of India's tribal hinterland. In 1947, Elwin described about the Bastar region as follows:

> "The great plain of Chhattisgarh stretches down past Raipur and Dhamtari in hot and dusty monotony till it spends itself against the hills of Kanker. Thenceforward the journey is a never failing delights; as the travelier movers towards the Bastar plateau the countryside breaks into song about him; he is greeted by hardy smiling woodman singing at their work, the skyline is broken by fantastic piles of rock; all around is the evergreen Sal forest. Presently he sees looming up before him a row of sharply-rising hills, the sentinels that stand guard before the country of the Ghotul. The white pillars mark the boundary of the State are soon passed and the long steep ascent of the Keshkal Ghat must be essayed. From the summit there is a magnificent view of the great sea of hill and forest below".

Bastar region is largely covered with dense forests and mainly inhabited by aborigines. Bastar is characterized with a very high proportion of Scheduled tribes and a very low proportion of Scheduled Castes population. The Gonds constitute about 64 percent of the total population and have various divisions and sub-divisions. The indigenous people of Bastar region are generally known as "Gonds" but they themselves called "*koitur*" the term Gond and Gondi denoting the Dravidian, non-literature languages spoken by Gonds in ancient anthropological and historical literature. The Gond of Bastar is only a few of the many Gond groups that populate the area covered by the present Chhattisgarh State (Haimendorf, 1979). The Muria and Maria Gonds of the northern and central parts of the State consist of several tribes. There is the Marias of the Abujmarh country in the north-west of the State who come down to Kutru and Barsur and who claim themselves consisting of several sub-divisions, others calling themselves *Meta koitur* or *koitur* of the Hill. Then there are the Marias of the Kuakonda tract, the Gonds of the Kondagaon tehsil who have immigrated from Dhamda, and the Gonds of Antagarh who call themselves *Jharian* Gonds. The Telugu Gonds are not considered here. The Gonds round about Jagdalpur occupy the highest position and the Abhuj Maria the lowest. *Koitur* is the usual Gondi word for a Gond. In the south the Gond calls himself a Koya (Brett, 1990). The local aboriginal like Abhuj Maria, Bhatra, Dandami Maria (Bison Horn Maria), Dhurwa, Doral, Halba, Muria etc., are settled in an around Bastar region since long. In addition to these, almost all the major communities of the region were living in complete unity with one another. Subsequently, the kings became instrumental in facilitating the settlement of different ethnic communities for various purposes. It should also be noted that, the primary king of present Kaktiya dynasty of Bastar Annam Deo himself belongs to Warangal (South India), who was being accompanied by groups of different south Indian communities. When he arrived there he established his kingdom in 1325 AD. Another king Purushottam Deo while returning from the pilgrimage of Jagannath Puri (Odisha) had brought some Brahmin families in the year 1408 AD to perform religious rites and rituals. Similarly, there is reference on one Muslim family which was entrusted to collect revenue. They brought some members of Sao and Behna communities to this place. In addition, the people of other communities came here from almost all parts of India and settled here for business, service purpose and a huge number of east Bengali refugees were also rehabilitated in the region by the Government administration.

The present study is an attempt to give account on the death practices of Muria, Maria and Bison Horn Maria, and their beliefs, customs, funerary rites, regarding the memorial monuments as well as the impact of these beliefs and customs on life in the 21st Century. The custom of erecting memorial monument stone in different parts of the world is prevalent on a large scale among the diverse communities from the Neolithic times. Long before anthropologist had discovered any of the crude stone monuments set up by primitive races of today the megalithic graves and stone alignments of Western Europe had been the subject of speculation by prehistorians, who without any references to ethnological material soon came to the more or less unanimous opinion that the majority of these colossal stone monuments of past times were in some way connected with a cult of the dead. With the extension of the field of archaeological research megalithic remains became known from North Africa and Western Asia, and already Fergusson described a good many stone monuments of similar type from India. But it was only with the work of P.R.T Gurdon, T.C. Hodson, J. H. Hutton and J.P Mills in Assam that the importance of living megalithic cultures in India was fully recognized. In Central India, mainly in the Bastar region, erection of memorial monument stone in the memory of an ancestor is still in practice among the Gond and its sub groups. A most comprehensive account has been provided by Elwin and Grigson. Particularly Elwin has described the funerary rites in details such as the origin of death, the idea of the soul, rebirth, divining the cause of death, bringing back the soul, and the methods of erecting memorials. It is amazing that today these practices are continued to prevail in much the same way that were observed by the British authors half a century ago (Postel & Copper, 1999).

The present study was conducted on three groups like the Muria (north-eastern Bastar), the Dandami Maria (Bison Horn Maria (plain south of the river Indravati to Dantewada), the Marias (Hills of Abujmarh) and the Raj Gonds (east-central Bastar).

The Hill Maria

The Abhuj Maria inhabits the entire Abujmarh Hills. Abujmarh Hills are one of the most remote and most backward areas in Bastar region. 'Mar' is the Gondi word for tree and according to Rev. Hislop this may be the origin of the 'Mar'. Even assuming this to be correct, the meaning of the term 'Abujmarh' remains shrouded in mystery. According to the commonsense interpretation based on Hindi, the word Abujmarh may mean 'the unknown highlands' (Abuj mean unknown). If this interpretation is correct, then it is clear that the name has been given to the land not by the

Maria but by the more sophisticated neighbours. However, Abujmarh is not the term by which the Hill Marias refers to their land; they call it *Meta Bhum* meaning the high land. The tract is commonly referred to a *Mar* by other people.

On the basis of the meaning of the word '*Mar*' Hislop interpret Maria as meaning 'Mar of the woods'. The name by which this tribe is referred to in the Scheduled Castes and Scheduled Tribes List (Modification) Order, 1956, is Hill Maria. This term is unknown to the people, like that the Bison Horn Maria.

The history, if any of Abujmarh is obscure and it is not known with any certainty if the Hill Marias are the autochthones of this tract. The habitation in Abujmarh is fairly recent and may be about a hundred years old. Also, in his opinion the Hill Marias not originally belong to this area but have emigrated from adjoining Kutru, Paralkot, and Ahiri tracts. The cause responsible for this migration is not known, definitely there are indications that the exodus, from the old Paralkot Zamindari took place because of oppression (Census of India, 1961).

The people who live in unknown hills are known as Abhuj Maria (Grigson, 1938). They are found in the Orcha block of Narayanpur district and adjacent blocks of Bijapur and Dantewada districts. They are mainly *penda* (Slash and Burn) cultivators; though they also practise incipient form of settled cultivation. They also do paddy cultivation mainly, depending on rain waters. This does not satisfy the needs of their families for the entire year and they collect Minor Forest Produces (MFPs) to supplement their annual food supply. Rice is the principal crop of the area '*kosra*' and '*kutki*' (Panicum Miliaceum) are the major millet occupying the second place. They worship Mata Devi, *Bhima-Bhimin,*

Bhangaram, Gram Devi, Dongur Devi, Danteshwari Maa on different occasions. They are divided with exogamous Phratries (a descent group of kinship group). Each Phratry is divided into several exogamous totemic clans. Members of all the clans under one Phratry are treated as *dadabhai* (brother clan). So they do not marry with each other. But they can marry with their *akomama* clans members (wife's clan). Clan is locally known as '*katta*'. Each *katta* has its own god known as Pen.

The Dandami Maria

The Dandami Marias or Bison-Horn Marias are originally a group of Maria Gond tribe who got a separate identity as Dandami Maria or Bison Horn Maria because of their special type of head gear and the Bison-Horn fitted with a basketry cap with a bunch of feathers and string of cowries used during dances (Grigson, 1938). The people are scattered in Dantewada, Bijapur Konta and Sukma regions. The people are divided into five exogamous Phratries or Bans namely *mariv, kurami, sodi, markami*, and *kawasi*. Each of them is divided into a number of exogamous totemisitc clans (*katta*). The kinship system is classificatory type by nature.

They worship the sun, the moon, stars and earth goddess or mother goddess. The people appease *Mawli* and *Danteshwari Mata* during Dussehra festival and they come to Jagdalpur and join the colorful procession. The chariot is slowly pulled by the Bison-Horn Maria people with the help of ropes. It has been observed that, both Hinduism and primitive cults take major part of the festival. During Dussehra the tribal deities are brought from their villages and are allowed to join the procession at Jagdalpur. The Jati Panchayat is traditional political system which is controlled by the *pedda* and assisted by *para mukhia*, *kotwar* and *ath paharia*, *pedda* is a hereditary post.

The Muria

One of the Scheduled tribes of Chhattisgarh state is found in the districts of Narayanpur and Kondagaon. They are mostly inhabited on the north eastern- plateau and adjoining areas of Kotri plain of North Narayanpur. The Muria are linguistically a Dravidian tribe. They live together with other tribes in the same village. On the basis of dialect; Muria is divided into three sub divisions. The north-western part has the western Muria and the middle part has the eastern Muria inhabitants both the sub-divisions speak in Gondi dialect. While who live in south-eastern part speak in Halbi which is the lingua franca of Bastar and its adjoining areas. Racially they belong to Proto-Australoid group. The word 'Muria' has been derived from the Gondi word '*Mur*' which means the 'Palash tree' (Butea Monosperma). Grigson has divided Muria into three separate groups:

(a) Jagdalpur Murias: the Jagdalpur Murias are scattered around the adjoining areas of Jagdalpur town. It is also noticed that the Jagdalpur and its adjoining areas do not have any Ghotul (youth dormitory) for unmarried boys and girls.

(b) Jhoria Murias: the Jhorias are found in the north-western parts of Narayanpur and extended towards Kanker region.

(c) Ghotul Muria: the Ghotul Muria is scattered in Kondagaon and Narayanpur districts.

The Muria clans are divided into five Phratries, which they call '*Vans*' a Hindi word. All the clans within the one Phratry are known as *dadabhai* or brothers to one another and all the members of each clan are *dadabhai* to each other. Marriage relationship in the clan members of the same Phratry is forbidden. The word used to describe the relation of a clan into which one can marry others daughter is *akomama* combination of the words '*ako*' which means a man's mother's father, daughter's daughter and mama, which means a man's mother's brother, his father-in-law and his wife's-brothers-sons. Every clan has its own distinctive regulations. The first rule is that no one marries within the clan or a member of clan that is related to *dadabhai*. Marriages can only take place between clans that stand in the *akomama* relationship to one another.

Muria acknowledge large number of deities in a simple and homely manner. It has a definite priesthood and a body of mediums who communicate with the gods while in a state of trance. It erects shrines and temples to the gods and builds small huts for the attendance. It consecrates every rural activity by sacrifice and a sacramental meal. The above descriptions suggest that Murias take a great interest in the domestic affairs of their gods; they are much better acquainted with divine than human genealogies. They are proud of the multiplicity of the Bastar deities.

As it is very known that Bastar region in Chhattisgarh has been reported to be a melting pot of races, and their socio-cultural tradition. The area is homeland of Muria, Maria, Gond, Hill Maria, Bison Horn Maria, Halba, Dhurwa, Bhatra Dorla tribes etc. tribes; it differs from other tribal enclaves in that there were, concurrently, other diverse traditions from surrounding civilizations and those who ruled the area. For Bastar region has a history as varied as that of the rest of India. It was a Buddhist enclave in the fifth/sixth Centuries A.D, raided by the Eastern Chalukyas, Cholas, Western Chalukyas and Hoysalas between A.D.

844 and 1150, and ruled by the Telugu Nagvansis from the 11th to the 14th Centuries. In A.D 1323, Bastar was conquered by the Kakatiyas of Warangal and became the largest Hindu kingdom and survived the next few centuries till its merger with the Indian Union in 1947. While the Gonds speak a Dravidian dialect, the lingua franca is Halbi of Sanskrit origin. The influence of the various dynasties is most apparent in the art of the region. Poster, M. & copper z. (1999)

One of the most remarkable features of Bastar region is that the tribals of Bastar still control their religious and social life with their age old tradition of laws. Most of the tribes of the region combine allegiance to the formal legal system of the Indian Constitution with adherence to their traditional or customary law in their civil, social and cultural trait. The maintenance of law and order, social solidarity and cohesion are matters of local control. The sanctions applied by a clan, tribe or linguistic group were usually applied within the group. There can be exceptions, as when more than one are involved, being linked by a common culture pattern or close trading links, or share a common sacred and ceremonial bond. In this regard 'Pargana System' still admitted in the region, consisting of many villages. The name of the Pargana is either on clan or place name. The Parganans are headed by traditional head, the *Pargana Majhi* (traditional political head). The social organization of Muria, Maria and Hill Maria is based on patrilineal clan; all clans are divided into *dadabhai* and *akomama* to each other that is either 'Wife clan or brother clan'. Marriage is prohibited within the *dadabhai*. Here some of the posts prevailing in a village, in Pargana level and their roles are given below. Somewhere they are important in their socio-cultural and religious life, which assist to perform their day to day rites.

Pargana Level

- The *Pargana Majhi* is the Pargana head.
- *Chalki* is the assistant who in the absence of Pargana looks after the Pargana.
- *Pen Majhi* (Religious head); he wields more authority to that of the Majhi.
- Clan deities also known as ancestral gods.
- *Waddai* is the clan priest.

Village Level

- *Patel* is the village head.
- *Siraha* is a Medicine mans as well as religious head and practices magico-religious performances.
- *Gaita* also performs like village priest.
- *Bhum Gaita* is a secular head assisted to worship *Bhum* (Earth)
- *Pedas*

Family Level

- *Dadabhai* (brother clan) and *Akomama* (Wife clan)
- *Hanal* deity is the ancestral deity of the concerned family.

In Bastar, a tribal controls their community and socio-religious affairs according to the customary law and treats it as integral to their culture and basic to their identity. These laws strengthen the communities' age - old traditions and bind it together through normative rules. For controlling their age - old traditions some hereditary posts are available at Pargana level, village level and family level, who manages the internal affairs of the areas as well as religious rites.

2
CHAPTER

MEGALITHIC TRADITIONS IN BASTAR REGION

The custom of erecting memorial pillars in different parts of the world is prevalent on a large scale among the diverse communities from the Neolithic times. But in Central India mainly in Bastar region, the erection of memorial pillars in the memory of an ancestor is still in practice among different tribal groups. Large stones with intricate designs engraved on them make the beautiful landscape of interior Bastar of Chhattisgarh. These stones are called megaliths in archaeological terminology. The art of erecting stone pillars in memory of the dead by the local aborigines dates back to the Stone Age. The Stone Age burial practice, has however disappeared in Europe, Latin America and many parts of Asia. But, the "grave art" continues to flourish in tribal pockets of Chhattisgarh's Bastar region.

Most of the Bastar Gonds - Hill Marias, Bison Horn Marias, Dorlas and Murias erect menhirs (*uraskal*) and sometime also dolmens (*danyakal*) as memorials to the death (Elwin, Chapter-XII), and the erection is usually accompanied by a feast and the sacrifice of a cow or bullock (Elwin, Chapter-XV). This corresponds closely to the custom of the Gadabas, the Khasis and the Western Angami Nagas, and here as there is the idea that the dead honoured by a memorial stone can render active help to their living kinsmen. The ritual accompanying the transport of a menhir provides another parallel to Naga custom. When the

Angamis drag a menhir to the place of erection, a prominent warrior in full ceremonial dress stands on it; Elwin mentions (Chapter -XV) that a relative of the deceased climbs on to the stone with a drum and sitting or standing on it drums while the men carry the stone to its destination.

A characteristic feature of megalithic culture in Assam as well as in Indonesia, Oceania and certain parts of Africa, is the interchangeability of menhir and forked wooden post of Y-shaped. Such forked posts can take the place of menhirs and are erected with similar ceremonies almost invariably connected with the sacrifice of an ox, buffalo or bison. An identical custom is found in Bastar (Elwin, Chapter-XII) and Elwin mentions that 'in any case' where a forked stick takes the place of the menhir, the fork is intended as holder over which the tail of the cow should be hung. The huge forked posts of the Nagas, some as much as fifteen feet high, do not have this purpose but on a recent tour in the Balipara Frontier tract Haimendorf saw Daflas fastening to a forked post the tail of a Mithun (Bos Frontalis) sacrificed on the occasion of a peace treaty. It is significant that forked posts, whose erection entails less effort than the quarrying or dragging of menhirs, are sometimes retained where the other elements of a megalithic culture have largely decayed. Thus the Koyas of Hyderabad put up miniature forked posts on graves during the memorial feasts and the Raj Gonds of Hyderabad erect a temporary forked post on the place where the memorial feast is performed as in Bastar the tails of the sacrificial cows are invariably tied these posts. Neither Gadabas nor Bondos set up forked posts and it thus seems these Y-posts constitute a link between Gonds and Nagas but not shared by the hill tribes of Orissa.

Menhirs should, among the Bastar Gonds, only be set up on the hereditary clan-land of the deceased (Elwin,

Chapter-XIII) and this tallies with the Nagas custom of erecting memorial monuments in or close to a man's ancestral village, attached to the village site, which remain the same through the centuries, being here much stronger than among the unsteady Gonds. Similarly the Gadabas erect their memorial menhnirs on the *sodor*, the stone placed in the center of the village. Large flat stones with a few erect flat stones in village centers or crowded places are called *Sodor* among Bodo Gadaba, Sano Poraja, Parenga Scheduled Tribes. The *Sodor* varies in size and in general is the sitting place where villagers assemble for rest or gossip. Children play around under the shade of trees of *Sodor*. A favourite place for memorial pillars of wood indeed also for menhirs is the side of a road or path that is constantly used by the people (Elwin, Chapter-XIX), and this reminds us again of the Naga hills where the stones stand near larger and increase their fertility and the fertility of their crops.

But parallels are not confined to the outward appearance and position of monuments and the circumstances of their erection; there is an essential identity of beliefs surrounding the megalithic monuments and memorial posts. Elwin describes (Chapter-XX) how the Murias believe that the dead man's soul comes into the stone or pillar, selected for his memorial and guides those carrying it to a place agreeable to the soul. This belief that the soul or part of soul substance of a man attaches itself to the stone is very common; the Angami Nagas see in the menhir a vehicle of 'virtue' which emanating from a person and adhering to the stone, benefits his fellow villagers and the fertility of the crops. The Bonds consider the dolmen memorial as the seat of the deceased and salute it white passing.

Elwin has made it very clear that the Gonds of Bastar imagine the departed as capable of both beneficial and harmful intervention in human affairs (Chapter-V), and this belief in the unity of the dead and the living is indeed one of the cardinal features of megalithic religion. Stone and wooden monuments are but the focal points of a constant communion across the threshold of death, and it is perhaps this dominant idea of the immortality of man and the indestructible bonds between those once united through ties of blood or marriage, which gave the megalithic *Weltanschauung* as we may we call this philosophy, an appeal powerful enough to carry it across continents and oceans.

Among the Nagas the characters of menhirs as memorials for the dead is eclipsed by their function as monuments in honour of the living erected in the course of elaborate feasts of merit. But the difference is more apparent that real; the menhir set up by a rich man in his lifetime becomes his memorial after this death. The Gonds of Bastar do not seem to have the custom of erecting monuments for any living man, but in the neighbouring Malkangiri Block of Orissa, the Bison-Horn Marias sometimes erected menhirs for men who had gone to work in the tea gardens of Assam. Elwin mentions that among the Bison-horn Marias of Bastar some men, anxious for their future fame, will prepare a stone to be set up in their memory after their death (Elwin, Chapter-XIV) and it is not improbable that the erection of monuments by the living in order to raise their on prestige many have grown out of some such practices.

Megalithic customs still practised in Bastar region and its adjoining areas in Andhra Pradesh, Jharkhand (Chotanagpur) and Odisha. The tradition of megalithic monuments erected in honour of the dead also continues in a very few pockets of north eastern states of India. Megalithic elements among the Korkus, the westernmost of the tribes with Austroasiatic languages, have recently been investigated on the tribe it appears that the square wooden posts with pointed or rounded top (*munda*), often elaborately carved, which the Korkus set up in the course of memorial feasts in honour of deceased relatives belong to the same category as the *biddiri* stones of the *mundas*, and the menhirs and memorial pillars of the Bastar Gonds. They have no connection with the grave, and only rarely do flat stones or pillars of stone take their place. Thus we see here a branch of a megalithic culture where stone has been almost completely replaced by wood. Symptomatic of the dilution of megalithic ritual is also the omission of the cow-sacrifices, elsewhere accompanying the erection of memorial posts and stones. Wooden posts, also called *munda* and closely resembling some Korku memorial posts except for their greater simplicity are erected by the Raj Gonds of Hyderabad in the name of individual dead. The animal whose blood must redden the post is a goat although cows are sacrificed in the course of the great memorial feast. It seems indeed that among these Gonds of the hill tracts between the Godavari and the Penganga, two different cults of the dead, each bearing traces of megalithic influence, have met and dove-tailed. For the erection of such a *munda*, a square pointed post of teak-wood, close to the place where the body was burnt is quite independent of the memorial feast held in the village; the latter includes the sacrifice of a cow, whose tail is tied to rough forked post, uprooted and discarded on the next day. Between these two observances for the benefit of the dead there is no connection, the sequence is optional and either both or only one of them may be performed for any individual deceased. While the memorial feast with cow-sacrifice points to a connection with the Bastar Gonds, the custom of erecting *munda* may be due to a different influence, traceable perhaps to the same source as that of the Korkus *munda* posts. The monuments to the dead of the Bhils seem at first sight to fall into the same order as the *munda* of the Korkus. The materials either stone or wood, but more frequent are flat memorial stones with a man on horseback carved in relief. The monuments stand usually in groups facing eastwards, but never near the actual grave or burning place. Only prominent persons are honoured by the erection of such a memorial, but the accompanying ceremonial is compared to that of Korkus and Gonds extremely poor, and Koppers comes to conclusion that the Bhils were originally non-megalithic people and that in their present form the Bhil monuments shows the influence of higher civilization of northern and northwestern neighbours, the Rajputs and Gujaras to whom they must ultimately be traced back. These are indeed not crude stone monuments of the megalithic type but must be viewed against the background of other forms of Indian tomb stones and cenotaphs (Haimendorf, 1945)

Before discussing the customs and type of megalithic culture it is necessary to clarify the term ‘megalithic’. Moorti defines as signifying “a socio-economic expression of burying the deceased in a grave which may/may not have a lithic appendage”. However, it is essentially unimpressive character of this lithic component with reference to the India ‘megalithic’ burials that has led to the term being considered as misnomer. Hutton (Census of India, 1931, Vol. I) described that a memorial affords a temporary dwelling for the soul “pending its operation as a fertilizer of the crop”. The underlying belief is that the spirits of wealthy men are endowed with the magical power to enhance the good fortunes of a community. Mahawar, an eminent ethnologist had reported more than hundreds of megalithic sites are reported from Antagarh to Bailadila and from Dantewada to Kondagaon, from Jagdalpur to Bijapur, from Jagdalpur to Bailadila and from Dantewada to Sukma. In the region, basically menhhir types (large standing stones) of megaliths are found. Earlier Gonds inhabited in Kanker area also observed this tradition but discontinued.

Types of Memorials

In the Bastar region menhirs are erected in memory of the deceased person. Presently the Hill Maria (Abhuj Maria), the Bison Horn Maria, the Dorla, the Jhoria Muria and Ghotul Muria are still maintaining their megalithic culture and customs in their own clan, as well as in then own territory. As a rule memorials are erected within the territory *(bhum)* of a clan, though active participation in the rituals of an ancestral village declined to great extent after the passage of a few generations (Postel & Copper, 1999). Therefore, the customs have been abandoned in certain areas and by certain clans. Two kinds of stone are erected. The upright menhir is generally called *uraskal.* The term is derived from *urasna* – to bury and *kal*-a stone. *uraskal* is the word most commonly used in Dantewada and in north of the State *kotokal (a place where the memorials are located, Grigson)* is more often heard. Elwin study on "Funerary Custom in Bastar State" reported that at Surewahi near Anthagarh, the villagers told about two hundred and forty menhirs of the memorial field which they call *khamakal,* sometimes the term *gatakal* is also used. In Sukma Zamindari, the Maria speaks of the *khutamkal.* In English *uraskal* is known as upright stone memorials.

The size of the erected stone is twelve to fifteen feet high, six-eight feet broad and one foot thick, sometimes thickness of the stone is more than two feet. The stone used by the Hill Maria are smaller than that of Bison Horn Maria.

The Jhoria and Ghotul Maria erect smaller stone, and Muria of Kondagaon set up little menhirs not more than one foot.

Elwin's observed that the menhirs are erected for men, women and children, and usually stand in long row by the roadside, near the village boundary, in the neighbourhood of the graveyard, or even in the village itself. Stone for men and women are put separately, and anyone in the event of a suspicious death has his menhir apart from others. The *uraskal* has a cloth tied on top, signifying that it belonged to a man, while the one next to it is wrapped around in the middle with a cloth signifying the woman.

In the region some clan do not erect the upright *uraskal* menhir, but deads are honoured with flat slabs of stone on four boulders. The upper stone is called *danyakal,* and it supports *Odiyal*. In the Kutru Zamindari, the Arki clan calls the upper stone *gariyakal*. Grigson reported that "the Birya-Marvi and the Kuhrami clans are the only two which always make *danyakal* and never set up *uraskal* stones; all the other clans, even in the Marvi and Kuhrami Phratries, and including the small or Chudala Marvi clan, erect *uraskal* stones. This is not correct. The Chudala Marvi clan in many areas in Konta Tahsil, for example and in the villages like Gogonda, Makapal and Koya Vekur erect both *danyakal* and *uraskal* memorial stones. The *danyakal* is indeed becoming more and more popular; it is supposed to confer a certain dignity on the family that has it and for some reason it is said to be cheaper. Other clans who sometimes use the *danyakal* stones are the Tati, Muchaki, Vetti, Hemla, Oyami, Birya Barse, Punem, Durro and Rawa (Elwin, 1945).

The multi panel tied wooden pillars, sometimes square or sometimes in round shape are erected by the Bison Horn Maria in memory of well-known or a wealthy men. In Elwin words "to have carved pillar in your memory is the Maria equivalent of being buried in Westminster abbey". Grigson identifies the wooden pillar - the term *urasgatta* (derived from *urasana* meaning –'to bury' and *gatta*-'a pillar'). The Maria calls the pillar either *munde* or madia *kambha*. A wooden pillar is commonly erected at prominent place along a highway or roadside. It should simply be near any road or path that is constantly used by the people. It is usually made of *saja* wood and is erected with ceremonies very similar to those for a stone. The pillars are often made by non-Maria, although the instructions regarding the patterns to be engraved are given by the Maria. Elwins (1945) described that "the pillars of Barse Marka Barrem and for Marvi Mass at Jabeli were both made by Anda Kalar of Potali. For making Barse Marka's pillar at Barrem, has sister's son gave one bull-calf worth five rupees, two rupees on bull-calf worth twenty rupees, cloth worth five rupees, two rupees in cash and daily food while the carpenter was working. The pillar took fifteen days to make." It has been observed that various animals like horse, crocodiles, dogs, replica of riding on a horse, men who are carrying pot of *landa* (rice-beer), man riding on an elephant, birds (pigeon and other small birds) and Bison Horn Maria dancers, etc. are carved in the wooden pillar for decoration. It has been tempting to suppose that various animals and birds carved on the pillars have some totemic significance. The people of the area say that they simply represent the ordinary objects of the case and are carved there to indicate some of the interests of the deceased man. Elwin reported during his field work that "each pillar in fact attempts to be a biography in wood of the deceased. We seem him important carrying the symbols of wealth and power and riding on a horse or elephant. It is seen the dancers that delighted him and the pot of *landa* (rice-beer) which never failed to give him pleasure. We are shown the knives and axes that he used; the animals that he saw or hunted in the forest. Author imagine that we should have been shown more of his agricultural interests had the skill of the carpenter been adequate to carving ears of wheat or fields of rice. On the other hand, the predominance of hunting scenes may suggest where the real interest of the Marias lies". It is important to notice that these pillars are closely associated with the megalithic culture of the Maria. Sometimes both a menhir and a pillar are erected; sometimes the pillars end at the end of a row of stone monuments.

According to the District Census Handbook, Bastar district *(Census of India, 1961, Madhya Pradesh)*, The Bison Horn Marias have a practice of erecting stones (menhirs), in memory of and for the appeasement of the dead. In Some cases carved wooden pillars may also be seen and an excellent example of these may be observed near village Dilmilli on the main road from Jagdalpur to Dantewada. Near Masenar village, there is at the end of a long line of menhirs a pillar in memory of a famous man, Kopa Dhurwa which has a carving of the old man wearing his jubilee medal. Such pillars attempt to be a biography in wood of the deceased.

In addition to the rows of *uraskal* there are several large heaps of stones, each surmounted by an upright stone. These heaps of stones are locally known as *biti*. Each *biti* commemorates a single individual. Relatives of the deceased contribute stones during the building of the memorial such structures, however are no longer raised owing to the expense and effort involved and the fact that cement cenotaphs (*math*) are more in vogue these days. In the region locally cenotaph is called a *math*, as is the painted memorial. Now a days these are made by concert and colour with wall paints. Recent years in the region, where the megalithic culture of the people has weakened or has disappeared, they made *math* or erect the flat slab of stone where the two sides of which are elaborately painted. Sometimes on the top of flat stone they decorate with pigeons made by wood.

Here before, the description of beliefs and death rites in the next chapter it has been important to know the responsibilities of clan member. The Maria and Muria tribes are divided into septs, each of which has a clan god called the Anga, who lived at the *Pen-Rawar* or Central headquarters of the clan. He is worshipped by the Pen-Gaita or Pen-Waddai and these priests are assisted by magicians, diviner or mediums known as *Siraha*. The basis of Maria and Muria family life is centered around between *akomama* and *dadabhai* relations. The clans are exogamous though sometimes divided into Phrataies. All the members of one clan or of related clans are *dadabhai* to each other and are *akomama* to the members of the clans into which they can marry. The relationship between parents in law is known by the Hindi word *Samdhi*. The father of my son's wife will be my *samdhi* and he will have many important duties at my funeral. Words used in Bastar in connection with death ceremonies are these. The dead are described in Gondi as the *hanal*, a word which as Grigson rightly says is 'a past participial form of the verb *handana*, "to go", "Departed" is thus a literal translation. Its Halbi equivalent is *dhuma*. The priest for condueting Departed affairs is called by the Bison-horn Maria as *hanal-gaita* or *hanagunda*. There is a hanagunda/hanal-gaita for each separated clan. The hanagunda/hanal-gaita has to tie thread round on the corpse. Earlier he hangs the tail of the sacrificial cow on the menhir.

In many Muria villages there is a small shrine for the dead called the *hanalkot* or *humakot*. Memorial mehnirs are *uraskal* which are erected in *kotokal*. *Kotokal* is a place where *uraskal* erected, locally known as memorial ground. Every clan has its own *Kotokal* within the village territory. It has been reported in the areas that if a person or family goes away from his clan territory/Village for employment or else, then he has to come to his clan territory/place to perform the rituals of memorials to the departed, no other clan members do not permit to do rituals in their clan territory place.

3

CHAPTER

DEATH CEREMONIES, BELIEFS AND ANTHROPOLOGICAL PERSPECTIVE

If any person dies in the tribal society mainly in Bastar region the members of the deceased person, friends, clan groups, neighbours respond promptly. The cultural guideline of the society or region determines the treatment and disposal of the dead body. Similarly, the period of mourning, beliefs, values etc. are passed from parents to each and every member of the society. This chapter deals with death rites, types of cremation, treatment of the dead, and belief of re-birth etc. The disposal of the dead body is based on the current situation, age factor, death from diseases, etc. as they sometimes cremate or sometimes bury.

Death Rites

According to the situation the Maria and Muria sometimes cremate or sometimes bury their dead. The Hill Maria cremates important people and the victims of wild animals and buries the rest. The Bison horn Maria cremates everyone who dies normally, though they too burn people who have been killed by tigers. They bury women who had died during pregnancy or child-birth, or any, who have died of small-pox or as a result of an accident. The Ghotul Muria buries important people and children, *chelik (boys)-motiari (girls)*, and the victims of small-pox. They cremate all others. All the Hill Maria clans lay the corpse face upwards with the head to the east except the Usendi and Gume clans who put the head towards the west. The Bison horn Maria and the Ghotul Muria also lay the corpse on its back with the head to the east. The "Muria of Padbera said that since we came from the east we put the dead with their heads to the east, East is "UP" and west is "DOWN" (Elwin, 1945).

In a separate description of burial custom Mr. Grigson has remarked that the Dandamis (Bison Horn Marias) do not burn their dead but bury them unless killed by tigers or dying from cholera, small pox and women dying during child-birth. Among them the *Kotokal* of the Abhuj Marias is known as *uraskal*. In some tracts it is found that no *uraskal* stones had been erected within the last 10 to 15 years because of the severe expense. Since the ceremony involves killing at least one goat, two bullocks and the provision of three of four *khandis* of grain as well as rice gruel and mahua liquor. It is of course expensive but in Mr. Grigsons opinion it is being abandoned more because of the Dandamis as they raise themselves socially and are forgetting their Maria customs than on account of the cost since the same people will entertain a thousand guests at a wedding. In connection with this a reference may be made to the remarks regarding the title "Marias" *in Chapter XII of the Central Provinces Report*.

Hodson, *1937 [India: Census Ethnography, (1901-1931)]* described that in the heart of the Maria Hills in Bastar burial is the usual thing but there are exceptions. They never let a dying person on die on a cot but lift him on the ground this does not applied to women, who, in any case are not supposed to lie on cot. They say that they only do this because they did not want him to fall off the cot in a convulsion. The corpse is burnt or buried with the loin cloth that was on it at death and all jewelry. If other cloths are in the house which the deceased wore, there are taken to the cremation ground or grave for burning or burying with the corpse or for hanging up around it. All his dancing clothes and ornaments, aces (not his bow and arrows) his *Godar/ Korki*, (digging tool) but not spears are buried with him or burnt with them; in latter case they often pick up by passersby after few days and taken into everyday use, no money is ever buried with the body. A house or portion of a house where a death has occurred should be shut up and not inhabited. It is neither pulled down nor repaired. It is considered that so long as it stands it will be a memorial of the dead. If the death is due to cholera or small-pox or suicide, the corpse is not buried in the regular burial place. Persons killed by tiger are burnet where they are found or where they are after the inquest, and should not be touched. Logs are placed under the remains and kindled. They have no *marmangal* (a cairn of stones from 1.5 to 2.5 feet high, surmounted by a flat cap stone) or *kotokal* stone (a place where the memorials are located, each clan having separate *kotokal*) and no dancing dresses or other property are brought to be buried with him.

Maria treatment of the dead (Hutton, 1931) is described as in Abujmarh Hills deads are buried. The bodies of *Gaitas* and *Pedas* and their old wives and mothers are buried in standing position. When a person dies, there is no beating of a drum to announce the fact; the statement in Russel (iii, 89) to that effect is not true for Marias but only of Dandamis, who had in the past not been distinguished from other Marias. The custom of beating a drum is however now creeping into Abujmarh from the Dantewada and Bhairamgarh sides, where the Dandamis predominate, and has reached Lakka and Karangul, but is reserved for men of higher status. The drum used is the *Turam* drum, it is beaten by boys of the village continuously from death till the body is buried or cremated, day and night. There is no special village drum for the purpose but in the smaller villages usually the only *Turam* drum is village property and kept in the Ghotul.

News is sent to all the *dadabhai* and *akomama* relatives in other villages and to friends as well. The funeral takes place when they arrive, on the 2nd or even the 3rd day. All the women of the village assemble and weep and wail in and around the house where the body is lying. They never let a dying person die on a cot but lift him on the ground this does not applied to women. Who in any case are not supposed to lie on a cot, but say that they only do this because they do not want her to fall off the cot in any death convulsion. They close the eyes, and straighten out the corpse, which is lifted on to a bier. It is burnt or buraied with the loin cloth that was on it at the time of death and all the ornaments. If other clothes are in the house which the deceased wore, they are taken to the cremation or ground grave yard for burning or burying with the corpse, or for hanging up around it. All his dancing clothes and ornaments, his axe (not his bow and arrows) his *Godari* (digging tool) but no spears are buried or burnt with him in the latter case they often pick by passersby after a few days and taken for daily use. No money is ever buried with the body.

The corpse, which is not washed or otherwise prepared but is carried out just as it was composed after death is carried out on a hurdle. The work of carrying it may be done by anyone, except a *Waddai* (clan priest), whether he is a relative or not. The hurdle goes first, followed by all the relatives and villagers, all wailing and beating their breasts.

If the death is due to cholera or small-pox or from suicide, the corpse is not buried in the common burial place, but in another place away from the common cremation place. Persons killed by tigers are burnt where they are found or where they are after the inquest, and should not be touched, logs are piled under the remains and kindled. They have no marmangal or kotokal stone are given not food at cremation and only burnt with them whatever is found with the body or at the spot where attacked, no dancing dresses or other property are brought from the deceased's house to be burnt with him. Both for burial and cremation most of the Marias place the body in the grave or on the ground with the head faced upwards towards the east and the feet towards the west; the usendis of Orcha and other villagers however reverse this. The *Waddai* ordinarily remains as a spectator, just like else there, but he must not touch the corpse.

If there is no doubt as to the cause of death, the following ceremony is omitted. But if a young man or woman dies suddenly for no obvious reason, then the bearers halt on the path just by the grave or burning place and stand there with the hurdle on their shoulders. The *Waddai* takes seven Saja (Terminalia Tomentosa) leaves and places them in a row on the ground, some 7 or 8 yards paces away from the corpse; one leaf represents the Earth or *Bhum*, standing for death through the displeasure of the village mother, the second represents death from sickness, the third death through the displeasure of gods and ghosts (*pen hanal*), the fourth death through the magic of a fellow villager, the fifth from enmity arisen from a quarrel or exchange of abuses, the sixth death from the magic of a wizard, witch or Siraha, and seventh normal death. The *Waddai* or if there is none, the *Gaita* or *Peda* strikes the earth three times with an axe and calls on the corpse to disclose the cause of its death. The corpse then impels the bearers to rush to one of the leaves and stand on it or else the *Waddai* first excites the corpse by scattering rice over it, till it moves its bearer to one of the leaves is changed, and the former process repeated. If in 3 or 4 tests the same leaf is always indicated, they are satisfied that the cause of death has been revealed. If it is witchcraft, nowadays they do not precede immediately to hunt for the witch, but a seed of suspicion has been planted that will grow in the dark jungles of their mind, and will sooner or later lead to assault or murder. If the corpse makes several mistakes, they do not waste further time and assume that the death was natural. They admit that in old times in which witch craft was pointed out as the cause of death, the corpse was next asked by the *Waddai* to point out the magician among these present at the funeral or in the dead man's village or an adjacent village.

Then, if it is burial the bearers bring the corpse up to the grave which is shallow only waist feet lift it off the hurdle and into the grave, with feet towards the west and face upwards. The senior near *dadabhai* relative then throws a clod of earth on the corpse head and says "This is all I can now do for you, and I give you my portion". He is followed in turn by each of the *dadabhai* close relatives who throw clods all over the body, after them five elders of the village who are distant *dadabhai* kin do the same and alter them any *akomama* relatives who happen to be present in the absence of any near *dadabhai* relatives, 5 *dadabhai* elders take the lead in the ceremony. Then earth is shoveled in from all sides. His wife's brother/any senior wife clan relatives (*erramtogh*) carried all his property to be buried with him from the house to the grave and place it in the grave by the head of the corpse as soon as it has been laid in the grave.

Over the heaped earth leaves are strewn over these logs. Then carved wooden posts are set up they are called *hanal gutta*, and there should be four smaller ones at each corner of the actual grave and two larger ones in front. The posts are roughly carved wooden peacocks on the top, and have been made ready beforehand by the villagers in the jungle near the burial or burning ground from *saja* (Terminalia Tomentosa) wood at the time of digging the grave. These posts having been set up at the foot of the two front posts, a little stone cromlech, known as *hanal* garya (ghost's throne) is set up by the dead man's *erramtogh.*, (If a woman is being buried, it will be her brother but not her husband kind). The *erramtogh* then pours a little mahua liquor on the ground near each post, and lays some rice on the headstone of the cromlech, on which also he has poured a little liquor. He then takes a cock, find twists its neck, breaking the skin as though to halal (cut its throat) it with his nails, so that blood may be sprinkled on the rice he leaves the cock here and no one eats it. Then he drinks some liquor himself and after him all the *akomama* relatives presents, then the *dadabhais* and then others present. The *erramtogh* also offers rice and *kosra* (millet) in a little basket to the *hanal* and an empty handi, small size. The food and drink are paid for by the dead person's *dadabhai* kin. Before the drinking of the liquor, but after the sacrifice of the cock, the *erramtogh* ties a piece of his own cloth and pieces handed to him by other relatives and others who wish to honour the dead to the boughs of an overhanging tree. A bamboo fence is then made round the grave except the two front wooden posts.

For a cremation the ritual is much the same. The pyre is prepared before hand, and the corpse laid on it; no wood is placed on the corpse, in the manner of Hindus. The *erramtogh* brings from the dead man's house a burning log and with it he kindles the pyre and the *dadabhais,* village elders and other *akomamas* each place a small piece of wood on the head of the corpse, just as in a burial they throw clods of earth, using the same formula. They do not pile any leaves or wood over the ashes, but leave them there in the open, with fence around them and then the usual *hanal-gutta* and *hanal-garya* (table-stone/cromlech) are set up. In some places, particularly on the Narayanpur side of the country no *hanal gutta*s are set up or only once. Also the mahua liquor ritual differs; after the earth leaves and wood have been piled over the grave and the *hanal gutta* (if any) and the *hanal garya* (if any) set up, the *erramtogh* takes a leaf cup of liquor pours a little from it over the earth above the head of the corpse, and drinks the remainder; this is done after him in turn by the *akomama* men, the *dadabhai* men and then by the women present. It is probably evening by the time that all this has finished but at any rate the next ceremony must take place at evening. Most people proceed direct to it from the burial or cremation, but a few forget their offering of rice and have to return to fetch it. All proceed to a spot by the roadside near the entrance to the village, and there the senior *akomama,* the *erramtogh* or next nearest *akomama* relative, builds a cairn of stones from 1.5 feet to 2.5 feet high surmounted by a flat cap stone; this cairn is called a *marmangal* (small crain). Then he and each of the householder's present places a pinch of rice or *kosra* (millet) grain on the capstone addressing the dead man's *hanal* by his name and saying that he gives him this grain to eat. Then they go home.

A house or a portion of a house where a death has occurred should be shut up and not inhabited. It is not pulled down, and it is not repaired too. It is considered that so long as it stands it will be a memorial of the dead. If man is rich enough to put a stone to the dead in the *kotokal,* without waiting to collect sufficient funds, he should do so after four days in any case mourning is observed for four days and no one goes to work. On the day after the funeral the house and the *angan* (courtyard) are cleaned out and the floors are leaped. If on the fourth day the son or heir of the deceased cannot afford to set up a stone in the *kotokal,* he goes to the graveside and bows before the *hanal garya* (table-stone/cromlech) and tells the ghost he is sorry, but cannot afford yet to put up his stone, and begs him to be patient and forgive him for the delay and not to harass him.

When he has enough grain and money collected to pay for the food and drink required he calls together his friends and relatives and they all go off into the jungle to look for a suitable stone. There is no ritual for selecting one they just take whatever stone they think suitable and one which will require only as many bearers as they can afford to provide with food and drink. The highest was seen in Abujmarh were in Lanka (iakka), where several 6-10 feet height. They drag out the stone and place under it several cross pieces of wood, the stone lying between two long and stout poles to which the cross pieces of wood are lashed to the stone lying is then lashed to the cross pieces and the poles are lifted on to the shoulders of the bearers up to 20 or 25 or even 30 in number, and the journey to the *kotokal* begins. At intervals they stop to drink as mahua which give them strength to bear the burden. They are given a meal on the way by the dead man's heir. So they arrive ultimately at the *kotokal* and deposit the stone on the ground at the selected spot. A hole is dug in the ground at one end of the stone, and then the stone if small is pulled upright by willing hands and held there while the earth is shoveled in. if it is big and heavy, ropes are lashed round its far end and used to pull it to a vertical position, while 10 men or so on each side hold poles across the top of it to prevent it falling over while stones and earth are rammed round its foot. When the stone has been erected at its foot a '*hanal garya*' (table-stone/cromlech) is made.

Around the Kutru side of the Abujmarh Hills the heir then comes up to the *hanal garya* (table-stone/cromlech) and squats down with his back to the stone. He takes small 8 to 9 days old chicken and holding it behind his back and never looking at the stone, *hanals* it with his hands and nails, sprinkles blood on the capstone of the cromlech and then pushed the body of the chicken under the stone, next he places an offering of rice or grain on the capstone. As he makes the offerings to the ghost, saying whether you killed by magic or by any angry *hanals* or gods or died naturally I know not but now I have put up this stone for you and you must wander no more. Stay here in peace forever and do not disturb your descendants. He then runs off, with his back still to the stone which he must not see, to the nearest water where he and all who have been present at the ceremony wash their hands and legs, and disperse to their homes. Men and women are present at the ceremony, but no one must look at it; all sit with their backs to the stone. Finally lays the ghost, and no further funeral ceremony takes place.

But until the stone is erected in the *kotokal* the *hanal* must be fed every year at the Nawakhani festival in the *hanal garya* (table-stone/cromlech) at the grave, not at the *marmangal*. Around Karangul and Lanka they say that they do not erect the stones brought to the *kotokal* for women and children, but leave them flat on the ground. Everyone believes that these stones increase or decrease in size according to satisfaction or dissatisfaction of the hanal. Around Orcha, Hikpulla, Ader etc. a cow or pig is sacrificed in the village, and portions of the flesh cooked are placed under the *hanal garya* (table-stone/cromlech), while the tail and sometimes a hood, are fastened by a cord from the top of the stone. There is also a regular feast, in the village afterwards at which the rest of the beef and pork are eaten, is dancing is organized there followed by arrangement of liquor. Needless to say this is a far more expensive procedure and many *hanals* there have to be content with *marmangal* cairns (small crain's), which they say frankly that they put up if they cannot afford a *kotokal* ceremony.

Hill Maria

They believe in regeneration after death. That is why a deceased person's name is given to the children. In village of a death has occurred in any Abhuj Maria home they send message to their relatives both *dadabhai* (brother clans) or *akomama* (wife's clans) members and neighbours. When some of them reach the deceased home they shift the dead body. Every member usually comes with a piece of cloth, rice and liquor. They do not perform bath to the dead body. Earlier they were in the habit of using branches of trees (Sal tree) to make bier now a days they make from bamboo. The relatives carry the dead body on the bier to the burial ground. Villagers dig a grave in eastwest direction. Before putting the dead body into the grave they go round the grave for 3 times with the bier and then put the dead into the grave, with face in upward direction. The man who digs the pit throws first clots of earth followed by other gathers mourners. Various belongings are also thrown into the graves. After the grave is filled up in shall stones are kept at the head side and another two at the leg side. They sometimes make fencing around the grave or sometimes they demark the grave by a line of stones. The mourners take bath and go to their respective houses. One of the most interesting things is that when a death occurs in a village the whole of villagers do not work till the final ceremony is completed. The male and female members of each family prepare food separately for two times. Next morning entire villagers along with bereaved family members go to see the dead body and they hang or tie the clothes of the deceased person to the branches of a nearby tree or on the fence around the grave. On this day stone is erected near to the village or on the road side in the name of deceased person. This is known as *marmangal*. At Jatlur or Orcha this is known as *tuming*. There itself they offer tobacco, rice, *mandia*, liquor, etc. On this day they sacrifice bullock, cow, pigs and cocks. Forelegs of the slaughter animals are hung at the burial grounds. Next morning villagers go the burial ground to see it for the last time. This is known as *amod adna*. They keep the *marmangal* for about one year and on every festive occasion they offer food there in the name of deceased person. Then they take out the stone from the road side and erect it on the hills in a line. So that their coming generation can know the ancestors of each and every family. Once in a year when they take new food they also offer the same to the ancestors.

Hutton (1931), reported that "In the heart of the Abujmarh Hills burial is the usual thing, but there are exceptions; thus at Tondabera (Neghalur Tondabera) the Neghalur cremate all their deads. At Lakka village (lanka) at the foot of the hills on the Kutru side they ordinarily bury their deads; but there and in the next village of Bodel, they bury the bodies of men in a standing position, such as *Gaitas* and *Pedas* and their old wives and mothers". Similarly, Grigson stated that "the ordinary rule throughout the Abujmarh Hills is to cremate the bodies of headman and elders of influence and standing and of their wives and to bury all others".

Bison Horn Maria

In the Bison Horn Maria, soon after a person's death his or her nephew climbs the roof and stand just at a spot below which the face of the deceased lays beat a drum for once or twice and climbs down and beats the drum at regular intervals. This is the method of conveying the death news to the people around. When the relatives and villagers assemble the dead body is taken out of the house.

When it has been observed and confirmed that the person is dead, the *anyemar* (sister's son) is called and he only performs the tradition of drum beating. The tiles of the roof were removed from the room of the dead person. Only those tiles are removed which is just over the navel of the dead person. The drum is beat in continuously till the cremation ceremony is not finished. The cremation ceremony is not done till their relatives are do not gather at home. During the ceremony, *anyemar* cooks and eat separately. The villagers believe that the procedures of drum beating after death are due to the remoteness of the houses in the village. Drum beating is the formal announcement for the death ceremony. After hearing the sound of drum the relatives and others gathered at home. Presently they are facing difficulties in continuing this tradition, younger generation don't want to beat the drum. People are getting education and they are not interested to follow this tradition. The new generations have opinion that this practice must be discontinued, but there are others who are in favour for continuing this practice.

On the cremation day, the dead body is bathed and massaged with turmeric and oils. Its toes are tied by piece of white threads supplied by the Mahara community (Scheduled Caste). They cremate their dead at the community cremation ground. As the pyre blazes the mourners leave cremation place and halt somewhere midway while returning, a liquor or Ganges water is sprinkled to the people who gathered in cremation ceremony. When they go back to the dead persons home, again in the entrance gate of house water mixed with turmeric powder is sprinkled over them. They are also anointed with oil. Some of the person goes back to the cremation place for offering black hen. Here if the dead person is male the neck of the hen is cut with an arrow and if it is female member, then it will be cut from sickle. In Gondi language, this ritual is known as *kor katla.* The process of erecting the memorial pillars starts after the rituals of *kor katla.*

When the dead body is carried to the cremation place, a child of the house is carried cross over the dead body three times or even seven times. It is believed that the departed soul, even after death he has same attachment for the family as he was alive. They think that after the cremation process is completed, the souls of departed are no longer in the home.

Next morning all go to the cremation ground to examine the ashes. If any portion of the body remains unburnt, the death is believed to have occurred due to magic. On the same day, the son of the deceased makes ritual offering of a chicken, food, grains and cow tails at the burnt pyre being back and by keeping his hands at his back side. This ritual is known as *Bisqutea Torenand*. On the 4th day, ritual known as *Tala Paitened* is observed. This marks the end of mourning and population on this day a monolithic on wooden memorial known as *uraskal* is erected in the memory of the deceased. This function is known as *urskaned* is erected. The Bison horn Maria believe that the deads are converted into ghosts. If someone dies during child birth she became an evil ghosts.

They are also benevolent ghosts helping the living in their day to day activities.

Muria

The Muria believe in re-birth after death. Soon after death they send news to Ghotul. Ghotul boys and girls go to inform relatives of the family. Relatives come along with a new cloth, grain, liquor etc. The oil is rubbed on the face of the corpse and new white cloths are wrapped, the wedge part of the plough is placed on the chest of the corpse. Then the women of the family perform the ritual before the corpse is taken out from the house for cremation place. The corpse is carried in a bamboo mat followed with beating drum accompanied by death song sung. In Muria, society the burial ground is located nearby the village boundary or in entrance of the village jungle. According to the types of death they decide, which type of cremation to be performed. The dead body is put in the grave with leg to the west side. Before placing the death body in grave, few banana leaves are spread. New cloths from the dead body are taken out and females' members pour mahua liquor near to the head side. After this they put some paddy and rice and body is covered with salt. The elder son or village *Gaita* put soil on the grave after this others one by one followed the same by male members. While the female members put soil into the Saja leaves one by one, as collected and put into the grave. After this all the mourners throw a clot of earth on the dead body. Many small pieces of stones are kept on it. They transplant *kichaumal* (thorny plants) around the burial.

When all the death rites are performed in the cremation and burial ground they return home and everyone rub mustard oil on their face and feet, for their purification. Some take bath also. This is known as *Lei Ushna*. Elderly persons request all the mourners with folded hand to take meal. On the same day deceased person's wife's bangles breaking ceremonies is performed. This is known as *Chuding Ukna*. In the same nigh elderly persons of the relatives along with deceased son go to a road crossing; keep rice and pulses in the *dona*. They prepare *palli* of rice and keep rice on 7 places for *Anal* (deceased person's soul) and sacrifices chicken. This is known as *Tum Kiyana*. Two people cover the cooking vessels and bring them to the house. Secondarily they go to the burial ground to pour mahua flower and put some money on it. This is known as *Vichand Dana*. First men and then ladies go the *vitch* (burial ground). From this day the mourning and visits are over. In case of cremation of the corpse, the corpse is rotated three times in wood and then body kept on the wood. All the relatives arrange wood on the body and lastly the son of departed parts burning of the dead body.

Siraha is the socio-religious fellow who is the capable to identify the causes of death. Next day of the cremation, Siraha along with some male members visit the burial ground in search of the cause of death. If they find the foot mark of a cow on the ash they believe that it will bring welfare in their houses and their cattle's and wealth will increase. The foot marks of the human specify that he was assimilated in gods. If the marks of tiger, snake, dog foot, then it is believed that the person's rebirth will be in amongst these animals.

During field study the villagers of Lasunhar, Narayanpur reported that on 15th day of the death all the relatives and sagas are again assembled to the deceased house. On that day they all go to the cremation place where the departed was buried or cremated. The *akomama* offer cooked rice and mahua in the name of departed and then back to house.

After return from cremation place, *akomama* keeps a new earthen pot in granary room with full of rice along with mahua liquor and some parched rice to the ancestral god. In forenoon all the sagas and kin members are served with liquor both *mahua* and *landa* (rice-beer) followed by a meal whatever is made in family. Sometimes this ritual is also done in 13th day of the death.

4

CHAPTER

PROCESS OF ERECTING MEMORIALS IN BASTAR REGION

The process and functions of memorials erection in the tribal groups of Bastar has its own specialty, which shows their unwavering faith in their ancestors. They believe that by honoring and worshipping their ancestors in this way, the ancestors are happy and pleased. They will protect them from any catastrophe that may occur in their life. The setting of memorials for departed soul is quite complex, no single person in the society can do this arrangement alone. He has to take help from society and their kin members (both *akomama* and *dadabhai* members). The *akomama* and *dadabhai* kin members are assembled at the appropriate time and date for functioning in erecting memorials. Such arrangements and function are mostly dependent on the fiscal condition of the family, if there is availability of money and other provisions in a family they do it in the thirteen or fourteen days after death. This type of provision is made by Bison horn Maria. Opposite of this, in Hill Maria, whenever, the family heirs have gathered sufficient provisions in the house is made. Almost similar practice is found in Muria too. In the course of study it was found that it takes twenty to thirty years to do this function. There is a general belief that these memorials (mainly stones) are increased or decreased in size according as their *hanal* is satisfied or not.

Hill Maria

The erection of a stone memorial entails considerable expense as it involves providing food and drinking to a number of people as well as making animal sacrifices. At the end of the period of mourning the heir, if rich enough, should proceed at once to set up a menhir to the dead in the *kotokal*. If he however, cannot yet afford to do so, he goes to the graveside, bows before the *hanal garya* (small crains/ cromlech), tells the dead man's *hanal* that he is sorry that he could not yet afford to erect his stone, and begs him to be patient to forgive him for the delay and not to harass him. It may take him two or three years to collect the necessary grain and money for feeding those who help him to find and erect a suitable menhir, (Grigson, 1938).

When the heir collects adequate money and grain needed for the erection of a menhir, he sends message to all his relatives and neighbours that he has collected money and grain and he wants to erect menhir. Accordingly all the clan members both *dadabhai* and *akomama* gather on the fixed date. They all go to the nearby forest or the spot for looking the suitable stone for erection. It has been observed that the size of the stone is based on the resourceful persons gathered in the spot where the stone is drag and carry to the erecting place. The Abhuj Maria attach several cross pieces of wood beneath the stone and tie a long thick pole to either side of it. Almost twenty to thirty bearers lift the poles on to their shoulders and carry it to the place where stone is to be erected. From time to time they stop and the heir of the dead man provides liquor to drink and at least one meal on the way. On arrival the stone is erected under the supervision of the *erramtogh* or the senior wife-clan relative present. After the stone has been placed in its hole and earth and stone rammed round the base, in many places a small cromlech (called *hanal garya*) is made at the bottom. The heir squats on the ground with his back to the menhir. He takes a chicken and holding its behind his back cuts its throat with the nails of his hand, sprinkle blood on the cromlech and pushes its body beneath it. Then still with his back to it he makes an offering of grain saying, whether you were killed by magic or the wrath of the clan-god and departed or died naturally, I know not but now I have put up this menhir for you and you need not wander no more. Stay here in peace for ever and do not worry your descendants. Then the heir still with his back to the menhir goes to the nearest pool of water followed by the others present and they wash their arms and legs and return to the village. Here the *erramtogh* sacrifices a cow or pig or both the cow is sacrificed generally in the room of the heir's house before the pot of the departed with the blunt side of an axe head and the words, I sacrifice this in your name: hereafter keep still and do not make trouble for us. The tuft at the end of the cow's tail is fastened to a loop of cord and they take it to menhir and place it over its apex. The heir then entertains the whole assembly to a feast of the sacrificed beef and pork and the night ends in dancing and liquor (Grigson, 1938). It has been reported during field work that the cow sacrifices is limited in spite of earlier times but now they are sacrificing more pigs in the Abujmarh Hills.

In the Kutru region, they do not erect stones for women and children but leave them flat on the ground. The stones for women and children, whether erected or prone, are always smaller than those erected for men. 'If a person is killed by tiger or other wild animals' Grigson, says he must be burnt, not buried, at place where their remains are found, or to which they are brought for the inquest. They must never be brought into a village...... No *marmakal* cairn and no *Kotokal* menhir are set up for him (Grigson, op.cit.).

Bison Horn Maria

The process of erecting menhirs in the Bison horn Maria differs from Abhuj Maria. Here the sister's son plays a leading part. Led by him a party of three drummers and a boy beating a gong and twenty to thirty men go out to the quarry where the stone has already been cut out or to some hill where a suitable rock has been observed. The sister's son touches the stone and address the dead man, 'In your name, ' we are bringing this stone ;let it be light let not the burden be too heavy. They place poles above and below the stone two or three above it, lashing them together with rope made of the camel's foot creeper. If the stone is very, heavy, additional poles may be put across it so that more bearers may support it. Then the sister's son with a drum in his hand climbs on to the stone and begins to drum with a new rhythm which goes *gul-gucha, gul-gucha, gul-gucha.* Some twenty men lift up the stone whistling loudly, *soor-soor –whee-whee* and sing it to and fro. Then they move towards the palace where the menhirs is to be erected, the drummers perform dancing and drumming in front, the sisters son beating his drum above. From time to time they put their burden on the ground and rest, and the sister's son has to give them rice-beer or mahua liquor. As they are being given their refreshment the sisters' son sacrifices a cock. He holds it by its legs and offers it a little oil in a leaf –cup asking the cause of death. He goes on reciting every possible cause and when cock puts its break into the oil he hits its head against the drum and so kills it. When the party bring the stone to the hole that has been prepared for it, the drummers throw the castor-sticks which may be made of any kind of wood. Before the stone is erected the *Gaita* addresses the dead……

> "You are dead and you must forget your father, your mother, your brother and your family. This is your house. Live here and do not trouble us or our pigs and cattle. We are giving your rice and pulses, and everything that you had at home, so that you may be satisfied"

In the hole which has been dug by the sister's son, the relatives put something or other, rice, small coins, rings or ornaments, whatever they can afford. In the region it was told, once the female relations of an old man threw bangles, beads and necklace worth at least ten rupees into the hole. Then the bearers unite the stone from its poles and all push and lift it into position. Earth and stones are rammed round the bottom and a small cromlech is placed in front. On this, stone offerings are made by the sister's son with his back to the menhir in much the same way as in the Abujmarh Hills. The women of the household come and put cooked rice and *haldi* (curcuma Longa) in leaf cups on the cromlech, and pour upon it grain, roots or anything that the dead man used to like when he was alive.

Then the whole party return to the house and one or more cows are sacrificed. These were probably selected by the dead man during his life time. The cow is tied to a tree and the sister's son first feeds the animal with rice and then knocks it over the dead with blunt end of an axe. If more than one cow is killed, the others may be killed by anyone. They remove the liver and cut it in pieces. Rice is prepared in the house of the dead and divided into four portions. The liver is divided into twelve and one portion of rice and three portions of liver are put into each of four leaf cups. Then these cups, with the tail of the sacrificed cow and a pot of rice-beer, are carried out in a specially made basket to the menhir. One portion is put on the ground for Mother Earth and the rest for the dead man on the cromlech. The tail is hung over the mehnir and the beer poured upon it. At the same time a little beer must be offered to the old menhirs. If this is omitted the ancient dead will be angry and will quarrel with the new spirit that has gone to join them. They all go to bathe and then return home for the funeral feast either by the bank of a stream in at the house. On this day only the relatives by marriages eat the beef; if members of the house hold consume it they would feel as if they were eating their own father's flesh. After a week, the relatives by marriage should repay hospitality by bringing beef for the household. The drummers have to sit apart and are given separate food. There is often a diversion caused when somebody standing in a joking relationship to the sister's son goes off with one of the shoulders of the dead cow. He suddenly springs out on the sister's son and nocks him over with it. This is regarded as very amusing.

Some Maria, not out of any religious taboo but purely from personal taste, eats neither beef nor pork; others do not eat chickens but pigeons; others again are vegetarian. For such people cows are not sacrificed for the menhir (the family may kill a cow for the funeral feast but this is not then offered on the cromlech). Instead, whatever animal or bird was particularly relished by the dead is killed, while for vegetarian rice cooked in milk is offered. Rice beer must be given both to the menhir and to the mourners. It must be made fresh in the room where death occurred and served with a gourd with a long handle that has been specially followed out for this purpose. Usually there is no stock of rice beer at hand and it cannot be made so quickly. The Maria then mix a little *mandia* flour (Finger Millet/Ragi) with water and give this instead.

The position of the drummers and the man who beats the gong is peculiar. They must all be related on the female side to the dead. They are regarded as outcaste for the two days of the funeral. They must eat separately, sitting on a separate mat, and food is cooked separately for them. They must not have any beef that day, but a cock is killed for them and they are given in with purified form. By the evening of the second day they are regarded as cleansed and are then allowed once gain to mix with the people, why this should be, I do not know. If for any reason in the course of the ceremony some rite or custom is omitted, the spirit of the dead man may attack one or other of the mourners in order to show his displeasure. For example, at Gadapal, Burka Peda told me that they once forgot to give rice-beer to the old menhirs and the insulted dead attacked his father's sister and she fell down in unconscions. They quickly gave both rice-beer and mahua liquor to all the mehnirs and she recovered. Again in Mahara-Karka one Kuhrami Eriya was hurled into the fire by the angry ghost and his leg was burnt. If this happens it is a good plan for the victim to run and catch hold of the broken bamboo poles of the bier. The *Gaita* pours water upon him and the angry ghost leaves him alone.

In Matenar village, (Dantewada district) Shri Nagdu Ram, described the memorial tradition in his area as follows:

> "He said that previously when some elderly persons died they were buried but since now we have started living with other people; we are therefore forgetting our rights and customs. We live with Rauts and Kalars etc., and I cannot understand why we are following this customs. We construct our memorial pillars with cement. Persons of other communities are buried at one common graveyard but we bury our dead in different places. If a person is old he is cremated and if someone dies accidently he is buried. He also said that if all the people are buried no place will remain for burial therefore we usually cremate our dead's. The people who belong to the same family or

clan are buried at the same place. For example Podyami, Banjami, Salam, Veko etc. has own graveyards".

In Bison Horn Maria, it has been reported after the cremation of the dead person, it will take some time for preparation of logwood for the memorial pillar. After the arrangement of logwood it will require time for smoothening or carving the objects. They take 8 days for male members and 9 days for female members. The maximum time is fixed and it is not more than 11 days. The next day after the cremation, rice is cooked at home in new earthen pots and it is taken to the cremation place and the whole cooked pot is offered in the name of deceased person.

During our field visit in April, 2016 at village Kilepal (Patel Para) of Bastanar block, the study team reported a newly constructed memorial pillar of stone, covered with dancing dress in the left side of Jagdalpur-Dantewada highway. Following communication with the villagers, it is found that a 45 years old woman 'Daiko" has lost her husband late Lingo Ram Poyam. In course of interview with 'Daiko" she informed that this newly memorial pillar was erected in the honour of her husband, he was dancer. His favourite dancing dress was covered on his pillar. It is belief that he is able to go with his dancing dress, and he may perform his dance in his new abode. This shows that the memorials are the biography of the deceased person in the region. The characteristic features of the deceased person are also with him after the death.

Some memorials were found near to Bastanar Bazaar, but the persons were alive. There is a question in mind that how it is possible. Yes, it is. A printed memorial pillar on the left side of road near to Bastanar Bazar at Nakapara was erected. The painted memorial pillar is very colourful, covered with stone shades. Following investigation in the village it has been reported that it is the memorial pillar of Koshu Benjami, and he is alive. He has erected his own memorial pillar, because after death his son may not show any interest to erect pillar in the name of his father. Therefore, he himself erected his memorial. This shows that, the younger generations are not interested to do these funeral rites. And as such the respondent is aware of that after his death, his son will not do this funeral rites. It is generally believed that of the last funeral rites is not done properly to the deceased person, he will be wandering one place to another. In the region it has been also reported that some families have made their memorials pillars for themselves.

Muria

Muria also observes the rites of erecting pillars for dead's in the honor of their ancestors. This ritual is locally known as *Kal khuta.* The function is done according to the capability and proper provisions in the family. If arrangements are made, they do this gathering with the help of their clan members. Muria tribe erects two types of poles both wooden and stone. Locally, if they erect stone poles they call them *Kal khunta* whereas for wooden they called them *Gata Khunta.* Here *Khunta* means "poles", which is either wooden or stone. The *Kal khunta* rituals are celebrated for three days. The day of the rituals started with the receiving of the clan relatives. On these days an elderly women locally known as *Pat Dokari,* in invited to sing Hanal Pata songs (Death/Burial songs). She sings songs in the name of the dead person. *Pat Dokri* is accompanied by her assistant known as *Rocheg* in Gondi dialect.

The ritual of raising the *Kal khunta* is completed in the third half of the second day. In this day a stone is buried (*Kal*) for the name of deceased person. The stone is called *Gudra* in their own language, considered an emblem of the deceased person and where they offer and worship. There is a belief of the family and their kin members that this place is belonging to their ancestors, and after death, all family ancestors reside here and stay around us and seed good and bad deeds of the life. It is also believed that if the buried stone (*Kal khunta*) falls, which shows that proper worship and care was not done to the ancestor and he had left this ancestor's abode and has gone to some other place.

During erecting of *Kal khunta,* they offer food and other items to their ancestors. As far as food is concerned, the women of the house take bath in the morning and start preparing food, on this day she takes bath but do not brush her teeth and reaming fasting for whole day. Keeps cooked food for her ancestors in *Hanaduma.* The main offering materials are *chila* (flat bread) from rice flour, lye, maize, paddy, and mutton (without salt) with local wine such as *landa* (rice-beer), sulphi (Caryota Urens), mahua (Madhuca Longifolia) etc. In the afternoon they gather to collect stone with their offering materials. The Siraha (Priest) of the village first performs the worship. As soon as the worship is done, *Siraha* out of touching the stone orders to dig it out from ground. *Akomama* digs out the stone from the ground, and after that family members wash the stone with water and apply turmeric and oil on it and also offer a Tarpan of liquor on it. Generally, the stone is wrapped in a white cloth, sometimes colorful new cloths. Then *akomama* carries the stone on his shoulder and goes to the ground where erecting process of his ancestors is being done. He erects the stone and worship and after that other family members offers

Chila (flat bread), Corn, Kochai Kanda (colocasia tubers), Paddy, mahua, oil etc. in the name of departed and desire to bring happiness and good luck to the family concerned.

The third day of the function, arrangements are made for a '*hatum*', which is a replica of a weekly market/*haat*. The environment of this market is full of persiflage among the kin members. Womenfolk gather here with some dishes from their homes and they perform the activity of selling these dishes along with stones, woods, earthen tiles etc., while male members mainly *akomamas* try to buy these things with a piece of stone, leaves etc. in the form of money. In this market-like replica, they take their souls of their deceased to their own homes by misleading the evil spirits and this leads to the farewell of their relatives. In this function the maternal side has an important role, the *akomama* (mothers brother) who performs all the rites as well as supported by the village *Gaita* priest, Mati Pujari, Deo Pujari, Pata singer etc. *Pat Dokri* sings folk songs in the honour of deceased person. There is a belief that those who die unnaturally are not included in the ceremonies. The priest worship his deities (*Gorka Deo*) and *Hanalduma* and try to know whether the dead rites have been done properly, and also if there is any deficiency. If any deficiency is found then they fulfills it and announce that the programme is completed. Farewell tribute to *akomama* and *Pat Dokri* and her associates are given with bronze utensils, iron rings, money etc.

In Muria society some clan groups perform the program of *Gata khunta*, which is similar to the *Kal khunta*, the only difference between these two only wood and the stone. The *Gata khunta* literally means a wooden pole. Two types of wooden poles are found one used in the wood of the mahua tree and the other in the wood of the Saja tree. The mahua

(Madhuca Longifolia) wood is used by Karnaga and Matra clans groups. It is believed by the people that from birth to death and in social and religious festivals, mahua (Madhuca Longifolia) wine has special significance. In each and every steps of life this is required and they are honoured to use it. Similarly, the *Khunta* of Aden (tarminalia tomentosa) is erected by the Mandavi clan groups.

5

CHAPTER

KAL KHUNTA (URASKAL) IN MURIA

The Muria like to associate the dead in all those activities which are dearest to them. Before they drink they generally pour on the ground a few drops of liquor in honour of the earth and of the dead. At every turn of human life, at every prayer that is offered and every ceremony that is performed, the dead are invoked. In this connection a study was conducted to document the functions of *Kal khunta* in the Narayanpur district of Chhattisgarh. Narayanpur district is one of the 27th districts of the State. It was carved out form the erstwhile Bastar district. The district is located in the southern part of Chhattisgarh and is situated at a height of 2000 ft. plateau above sea level. It had a population of 14, 11,644 in Census of India 2011(including Kondagaon district). There are 572 revenue villages in district. The district comprises 70 percent of the tribal population, which is 26.27 percent of the total tribal population of State. The district is the land of great Muria tribe which is world famous for their dormitory system (Ghotul) and the Abhuj Maria, one of the Particularly Vulnerable Tribal Groups (PVTGs) of Chhattisgarh. Besides these there many tribes are inhabited in the district. The tribes of the district are known for their unique and distinctive tribal culture and heritage all over. Each tribe has their own distinct culture and enjoys their traditional life style. The documentation of *Kal Khunta/ Gata Pakhna* as well as the rite of "bringing back the soul" has been covered with full of enthusiasm. Three villages are reported in year 2014-2015 that they are preparing for *Gata Pakhna/Khunta*. These villages are Sulenga, Lalsuhnar and Devgaon situated in Narayanpur development block.

First two villages namely Sulenga and Lalsuhnar where it had been decided to do the functions of *Gata Pakhna*. A question arises in the mind that why and when they performs the functions of *Gata Pakhna*. The Muria elder told that when they have sufficient grains, money and all other things sufficient in the house, all the dead man are summoned for a feast (memorial feast). Sometimes the relations are warned by a dream that the spirit of the dead is dissatisfied and, that they must do something to appease and honour him. In this regard, a formal meeting with the clan members residing in the village are gathered in a meeting place. Earlier they used to gather in Ghotul house. They fix the date and month for the functions; on this day they also calculated the amount that will be required in the function, accordingly they distribut same amount to every clan members (from same clan) that has to participate in the functions. Locally this meeting is known as *Vadki Kal*. When the date and month is fixed at *Vadki kal*, the invitation is given to the clan members to participate in functions with proper contribution, which has been fixed. In the Sulenga village it was fixed in the meeting that every family whose members are dead, contribute one goat, one bullock, two Khandi rice, five liters mahua liquor etc. These items for one dead person, if a family having two or three dead person, they have to double and triplate their contribution.

Invitation

The whole and sole responsibility of the functions is assisted by the Patel (village headman). When the date is fixed for the rituals invitation is made by male members of the family. It is his responsibility to message the family; he goes with a bottle of liquor with him to invite the invites. Both the family head and messenger take little liquor from bottle as for acceptance of invitation as well as in the honour of dead. Clan member praised his clan-god that, after so many years they have collected sufficient provision in the house, which he collects for the memorial fest. Earlier this process of invitation was made by *Chelik* (a boy member of Ghotul).

Essential person for function:

During the function of *Kal khunta* there is bare need of some essential persons who assist the function as and when they are required. Everyone, has its own role. These essential persons are Mata pujari of village, Dev pujari, Gaita, Bhandari, Guru Mai (Pat Dokri), Pat Dokra, Sirha, and members of *dadabhai* and *akomamas.*

Preparation

Preparation of the function is more important aspects of this function, because thousands of people gather in the village for this function. One day before all the people assemble of both *akomama* and *dadabhai* relatives reach in the village. The term *akomama* and *dadabhai* are described by Elwins as follows:

'All the clans within one Phratry are *dadabhai* or brother to one another and all the members of each clan are *dadabhai* to each other. The word used to describe the relation of a clan into which you can marry your daughter is *akomama,* a combination of the word *'ako'* which means a man's mother's father's, daughter's son and daughters daughter (all of whom will belong to a different clan in a different Phratry) and 'mama', which means a man's mother's, brother, his father in-law and his wife's brother's son (who will again of course be members of different clans)'.

Every family in the village make proper shades from Sal (shorea robusta) poles and *chind* or wild date palm (phoenix sylvestris) leaves in the courtyard of the house. A common temporary shade is made for gathering the items which are contributed in *Bhandari Ghar*. The in-charge of this temporary shade is known as *Bhandri.* He has to document all merchandises which are contributed from Clan members and fully recorded in his dairy. Besides this a big hearth is also dug out for cooking purpose. A bamboo stand is also made for collection of cocked rice. Big earthen pot is used for pulses and cooked vegetables. All the members who participate in the functions directly come to the temporary *Bhandari Ghar* (or temporary shade for collection of items). Female members mainly elderly welcome with traditional way with cleaning of feet with water and give an *arti* with their traditional lamp. After this she applies a mixture of oil, rice and turmeric on the both side of the face and forehead.

First day

Some of the relatives come in the home very early in the morning; similar process was followed in the first day of the function also. The young generations of the village both male and female prepare the hearth for cooking eatables things. The fire is burnt in the big hearth, which was earlier dug by the villagers. Here cooking of rice, pulses, meats, vegetables etc are prepared on regular basis on the supervision of *Bhandari.* In the first they the relatives, remain ready for the function. At 11.30 am two elderly ladies are invited in the function, the villagers told that they are *Guru Mai*, and they sung *Hanal Pata* in the name of deceased person. Almost similar process is followed to welcome them.

During documentation it has been reported that in Sulenga village that the functions of 35 deceased persons are done, where 16 are female, and 19 are males. The names in female group are- (1) Sukhmati (2) Radhika (3) Gorse Bai (4) Bajaai (5) Manbatti (6) Matri (7) Fulma (8) Bhajji Bai (9) fulari (10) Rajbatti (11) Kondi Bai (12) Sambatti (13) Gashni (14) Rajbatti (15) Bajni (16) Agantis. Similarly in the male groups are – (1)Mahruram, (2)Sonsai (3) Chaitsai (4) Ramesh (5) Punauram (6) Shyamlal (7) Rajauram (8) Manglu (9) Pagguram (10) Mnehar (11) Maniram (12) Pigluram (13) Singluram (14) Mahruram (15) Kamlesh (16) Laxman (17) Birjuram (18) Pahadiram (19) Ram. All the above deceased people belong to Gaita and *Mata Pujari* family. This ritual is conducted after 20 years.

The list of deceased persons is given to Guru mai and then they sit together with other female folk. The family member give a small pot full of mahua liquor to be and the *Hanal Pata* song is started by the Guru mai followed by other female members. Sometimes Guru mai is also called as *Pat Dokri*. Guru mai takes each and every deceased person's name one by one and after starting the song one drop of mahua liquor is given to *bhum* (Earth) in the name of deceased person. The relevance of the song is very important, because when a song is once started, it will be closed in third day of closing ceremony. It has been reported that in Sulenga men do songs goes on for more than 72 hours, in the name of deceased people. It is very difficult to identify the songs for deceased people. Because every time they sing a new line, that is somewhat in natural.

More than a thousand of kin members (both *akomama and dadabhai* members relative members) participate in the function. This is the time that they are waiting for more than 20 years. And they have to satisfy their deceased person at any cost. In village every where, the kin members and villagers are found in very jubilant mood, there is an enjoyment and they pass the time on singing and dancing with their traditional musical instruments like *mandari* (dhol) and *Todi* (hunting horn). In the evening more kin members and villagers are found join in the celebration. It has been also observed that the old generation shows much more eagerness, and enthusiasm than the new generation.

The division of work is more prominent in the function and was extremely decisive in the proper management of the ceremony. A gathering of thousands of relatives, and their proper reception in the village are vital. They are coming to satisfy their deceased person after long times. Female members collect leaves from forest for preparation of plates. The leaf plates are made of Sal leaves. Three types of leaf plates are prepared which are used in the function. These are *Gato dapa* (used for rice eating), *Pula dapa* (used for vegetables and pulses) and third one is *Java dapa* (used for drinking materials). Sometimes, according to the area the name of these leaf plates may vary. The first day of the function is all about the singing of *Hanal Pata* and Ghotul *Pata* and preparedness, arrangement of essentials to be used in the second day of the functions.

Role of Singing

In Muria tribe the role of singing is very important. On the first day of the ritual the family members of the dead person gather in the said house for celebrating the rites. On this day all *akomama* and *dadabhai* come with their gifts and contribution. In this day *Pat dokri* and *Pat dokra* come to the house where the rituals are to be celebrated. One member of the family who comes to celebrate the rites worships the *Hana pot* and Ghotul *Pata* and at same time the families of *akomama* start beating drum and ask the female members to sing *Hanal Pata* and the Ghotul *Pata*.

Hanal Pata: Hanal Pata "a song connected with death", mostly in Gondi language. The Hanal Pata song is used during the funeral ceremonies and at the time of erecting menhir. The song is sung by a group of Pat dokri or Pat dokra. Elwin described that some of the song, are sung according to the situation to be visualized in which the *kotokol* stone is erected at the same time that the *jiwa*/ soul is brought to the house. Sometimes song is sung during the bringing and erecting of the stone; it is interesting to note how closely life, love and death are allied, in Muria thought, which regarded them as a single process. The bulk of this song is indeed about life, and only at the tragic end of the singers' discourse of death. It has been reported that the *Hanal Pata* song is all about the details of ritual and relationship, and on the practical duties and expenses of conducting a funeral or memorial service. The line of song is very innocent and simple but it is very important to them. Here some of the lines are sung by the *Pat Dokri* during the rituals related to bringing back the soul in to the house. The song is continuously sung until the whole procedure is reached up to the *Hanal* room. They offer mahua liquor in the name of family ancestor and include the departed soul into their ancestor pen. The song is continuously maintained, for three days (almost 72 hours). It has been reported that the continuity of the song has been maintained with constant supply of mahua liquor to tinplate them going. This is essential, as a slighted spirit is supposed to strike down the singer. Some of the lines are transliterated in English word as follows:

"Go in hanal go inside,
So many days you are wandering,
You were in the forest for long, now come to hanal, come,
You are gone through several pains to sustain yourself,
You have done lot of things, now you are hungry,
You were in the open crop fields, now comes hanal, come,
You are wandering for so many days,
You were at the hills and forest,
You were hided in the stone and earth,
You are tired moving around, now go inside,
You are hungry and thirsty, now go inside.
Go in hanal go inside".

It has been observed in the field that, the line, of song is changed every time, which is very difficult to identify that what line she is singing. The flow of the line is natural. As the singing of the *Hanal Pata*, the dead are not merely remembered, but are welcomed with affection and respect. The main focus of the song is to unite the ancestors for survival of the Clan group, which is associated with *Bhum* (Earth).

Ghotul Pata

Previously the Ghotul Pata song used to sing by all inside the Ghotul (youth dorimotry). The song is sung by one and two person, others sung in chorus. The Ghotul Pata is sung by male members. In Muria, if there is a funeral ritual there is a special type of drumming, which denotes a death in any family in the villages and their funeral rituals is happening.

Kaufmann, (1960) described "Mention must be made of a particular type of song which may call 'instructive'. The song teaches a particular craft, for instance, fishing, or husking rice, etc. Many of the songs I took down have no words but use instead meaningless syllables such as "re, re, lo, yo, re, re, la," sometimes also "le, le. All songs have been notated as they sung, no melody has been transposed. Repeat signs mean that the melody is repeated over and over again, sometimes, as already mentioned, for a period of long as fifteen minutes. If not otherwise stated, the songs are sung by the whole group."

Second Day

The second important in the function in the ceremony is fixing a stone in the burial ground. The first half of the day is slip out with the gathering and arrangement of materials which has been used in the afternoon. This work is done by female members of the family. In this day the female members take fast and cooked food for their deceased person (food of *hanalduma*). The food is prepared in a new earthen pot. Flat bread of rice flour (locally known as *Chila*) without salt, along with parched rice, maze, paddy, turmeric, oil are kept in a bamboo basket. Which is offered in the name of deceased person during the fixing of stone.

In afternoon, the relatives are found gathering, where the stone has been selected. In Sulenga the place where stone is selected is named as Gudra Gagga. Siraha of village offer puja in this place, and direct to choose the stone. Then the *akomama* dig out the stone in the name of deceased family, stone is wrapped with white cotton cloths. Same procedure is followed by *akomamas.* Only the *akomamas* hold rights to pick up the stone. The stone is cleaned with water and they apply oil and turmeric then pour some liquor to it. The application of oil and turmeric represents the second weeding of the dead. Seeing this, all the family members get emotional, they start crying and start to remember him. After this they take the stone, into the place where the stone is to be fixed. The *akomama* is the man who picks up the stone in his shoulder and place in the fixing point. He digs the earth and fix the stone. The home made bread of rice flour, parched rice, maze, paddy, turmeric, oil, money and liquor are offering materials to the fixed stone. All the *akomama* and *dadabhai* relatives follow the same process, they also offer new cloths and money accordingly to the gender of deceased person. Money and cloths are gathered by the daughter or sister-in -law of the family, they have rights on it. After offering ceremony to every family is over all return to their house.

Third day

The third day is all about the farewell of relatives who have participated in the rituals. They organize a mock market which is locally called '*Hatum*' or Bazaar ceremony. They perform in an open place ground in evening. The female member of the every family cook some sweets and rice flour bread and keep inside the basket and gather in the mock bazar palace. They putt natural things like a stone piece, old cloths, broken roof, mud tiles, plastic etc. for sale in the bazar. And male members buy with broken piece of earthen pot instead of money. The purpose of this day is to bring the soul in his house. In this sequence it is taken care that bad soul does not get inside their houses in no way. The reason behind it is that; good soul is rotate in the mock bazaar, so that the bad soul cannot inter their house with good soul. Some of the villagers opined that it is a time that the souls of the dead are supposed to mingle with the ancestors. The activities of the Bazaar were carried out in a light hearted manner and everyone participated in the revelry. Same day in the evening the farewell is given to all the relative member and thanks givien to *akomamas* whose role is vital in the function.

The function is varying from village to village and even time to time. Elwins described that "in some village in the Kondagoan Tahsil the Maria go to the nearest Bazaar to buy parched rice, gram, and liquor. They walk round the bazaar scattering the rice and grain and then visit the grave of the dead. Here they eat and drink a little and go home, saying to the spirit of the dead, 'Come home with us'. They go into the room of the Departed and it is believed that the *jiwa* follows them.

The main purpose of ceremony is to maintain customs, beliefs and structured pattern of the society in the name of departed person. Muria belief in immortality, or at least in some kind of survival after death, is bound up with the idea of the soul. When a man dies, his fellow *hanal* take his jiwa to Mahaprabhu. After the proper greetings, Mahaprabhu says, 'Go and see what your relatives are doing. If you are satisfied and all the ceremonies are properly performed, then return here." The jiwa goes and sits on a tree near the village. When funeral rites are properly concluded, comes the living of Mahaprabhu who then says, "What good, what evil you had done? How many men had you beaten? From whom you borrowed and not repaid?" if the man dies with a large debt unpaid his jiwa is not allowed to mingle with the departed but is sent in the form of a bullock to his creditor's house. If a man has beaten many of people Mahaprabhu tie him up with a rope and hang him upside down and beat him on the buttocks. He is punished like this for twelve years and then sent back to earth as a man. But good men mingle quickly with the departed; they become gods (*deo*) and mingle with the gods.

The soul of the dead man is supposed to be living outside his home and must be brought back. Therefore, the jiwa is brought home after the erection of a menhir. The above discussed ceremonies are very expensive; therefore the families are forced to postpone it to a later period. When sufficient provisions are collected in home, some families are reported in the area about organizing their megaliths for their ancestor after the death of 30 years. It has been also reported that in Binjhli village of Narayanpur, eight families had permanently migrated to Maharashtra in the year 1970. But their family members came to village in 2001 to erect the memorial stone for their ancestors. This is a common character in the region. Every clan groups are tied with their ancestors. He has to do, or participate in the said memorial feast for ensuring the survival of their clan groups and strengthening their roots within the *Bhum* (Earth).

6

CHAPTER

IMPORTANCE OF MEGALITHIC PRACTICES AND PHILOSOPHY

Every tradition and culture has its own significance. The study of megalithic practices in Bastar region gives ample information about the death rites, beliefs and the philosophy of life in the communities associated with. For the sake of their existence in the hills and forest areas of Bastar region they are not forgotten to practice their indigenous cultures and rituals where the ecological resources have a great role. The deep rooted belief in the survival of supernatural power also exists to influence each and every step of their life and these belief systems gives them power to fight for survival. It is best suited for their existence. All have their own way of doing almost everything, right from childbirth, rearing, marriage, death, religious rites, festivals etc.

In the present study three groups have been taken for study where they continue their memorial practices. These are Hill Maria (Abhuj Maria) of the Abujmarh Hills, the Muria of northern and northeastern Bastar, and the Bison horn Maria who occupy the plain south of the river Indravati, roughly between Dantewada, Jagdalpur and Sukma. Megalithic practices seem to connect the entire community into oneness by tradition, which leads to unity in social and cultural spheres. The people of the region are controlled by the rules and customs of their society. The Earth (*bhum*) is the ultimate source of their life and power. The fundamental relation between the Earth, the clan-god and the village Mother….. is that the clan god is the Earth in its dealings with the clan, and the Mother the Earth in its dealing with the village (Popoff, 1980). Clans are both unified and separated by clan deities, more broadly "ancestral deities", displaying a continuum of conception and conceptual transformation culminating in the all-inclusiveness of the Earth, specifically the Earth Goddess *Tallur Mutte* among the Muria, *Tallin ochur* among the Bison horn Maria and *Talo Dai* among the Hill Maria. These are only the more generic names among many for the supreme female deity, and there are as well many, refractions which occur localized contexts such as to be represented as "Village Mother".

Social organization in all three group is based on patrilineal clan exogamy, all clans being either *akomama* or *dadabhai* to each other, that is either 'wife clan' or 'brother clan' the system taking on a moiety like character with a patrilocal, bilateral, cross-cousin marriage ensuring as egalitarian bias. Spatial organization of social groups follows basically two patterns; Hill Maria clans tend to preponderate each to an entire village, a group of agnatically related clan-village forming a 'territorial brotherhood' (Popoff, 1980), much more densely populated, Bison horn Maria areas contain non-nucleated villages with plural clan residences, although bounded within territorial link to a funding clan. As people believe that social relations are founded on 'territorial rather than hierarchy' by a clan god who is generally known as *Anga Dev*, or *Pat Deo*.

As a rule, memorials are erected within the territory (*bhum*) of a clan, though active participation in the rituals of an ancestral village. The association of the dead (*hanal*) with the clan-god is seen not only in the custom of erecting menhirs in the clan *bhum*…., but also in the Muria practice of taking the *jiwa* (soul) from the house to the *hanalkot* which is always connected with one special clan. The small pot which serves as a repository for the soul is quite distinct from the pot of the departed which is kept in the store-room or granary of the houses of the Muria, the Hill Maria and the Bison-horn Maria. The significance of this practice lies in the belief that the ancestors have the power to ensure a good harvest, especially, if they are regularly propitiated. In fact, the dead's are invoked during all important family occasions, as if they are concerned in the birth of a child or marriage. The protectiveness of the dead in the house and their influence in daily life of the concerned family renders them, "the guardian of the rules of taboo" thus effectively curtailing the infringement of social norms, (Postel & Cooper, 1999).

Hutton, (1931) opines that a memorial afford in a temporary dwelling for the soul, "pending its operation as a fertilizer of the crop". The underlying belief is that the spirits of wealthy men are endowed with the magical power to enhance the good fortunes of a community.

Religious beliefs and Megalithic

Troisi, (2000) has written that "belief and rituals are invariant factors in all religions. Rituals are rationalized and made effective by beliefs. It is only by considering religion as mode of action as well as a system of beliefs that the living meaning of both rituals and beliefs becomes evident". In the tribals of Bastar the beliefs, rituals and practices are associated with their life, which is the basis of their life line. According to their faith and belief, they perform their religious activities. For these, there are some places have been established in the name of their deities. It has been commonly seen in every village in the Bastar region. In village, *Devgudi, Anga Dev Gudi, Sheetla Maa*, etc. are found. These are the places of their worship and regarded as sacred places. In Bastar the tribals believe in ancestor worship. Accordingly, as per their clan groups they worship their ancestor. For fulfilments of their worship helping hand is required. These are known as *Mati Pujari, Deo Pujari, Siraha, Gaita, Waddai* etc. who are sacred specialist in the area. In spite of this during the ancestor worship in relation to the erecting memorials, the male member as head of the family is responsible for this ritual, accompanying with their *dadabhai* and *akomamas* kin members.

Role of Clans in Megalithic practices

It has been reported in the field area that the tribal society of Bastar is strongly associated with their clans. The roles of clan members (both *akomama* and *dadabhai)* are very important in their every sphere of life and after death they follow the rule of clan territory. There are special hills and forests where each clan gets its wood or stone for erecting memorials to the dead and for the clan gods. Elwin reported that at Paria the Sori clan brings its *danyakal* stone from the Wiskimeta Hill, similarly at Kokori, the Netmai bring their stones form Chapadaongri, the Maravi from Mahadeo-dongri and the Kalo clan of the Ghotul Muria village of Mahurpat used to fetch their *kotokal* stones from Boga in Kanker State.

In Bison horn Maria, they offer *kosra* (millet) and broken egg shells to the Earth *(bhum)*, and they say 'O Mother Earth, 'do not trouble us; we are giving you kosra and egg shell in place of the stone we are taking from you" after this they cut the stone. They pour water or a soup made of *hirwa* (glycine hispida) pulse on the stone and pile logs and branches above it. Then they fire these and when the stone becomes hot enough they again pour water along the desired line, and break it with their digging sticks. When it is sufficiently cracked, they praise the slab out with poles and digging - sticks. The process of cutting of stone and laid ready to erect in a proper place is very costly. Almost twenty to thirty people are required for this process. The stone is as big as twelve to fifteen feet long and four to five broad. It takes lots of time and money, because every person who is associated with this they must be honoured with mahua drink/*landa* time to time and have a proper meal for them. It has been also reported that some healthy person also arranged their own stone cut out and lay ready to be set up in his memory, while he is still alive. It shows that some of the people are seeing the process of cutting stone is very difficult and after death he wants big stone should be erected in his memory. So they prepared for his own funeral, though he was well and healthy.

It has been also reported that the stone is erected in their *katta* village. Here *katta* mean clan village. Villages are made of a number of hamlets or para to one or some of para or hamlet belong the descendants of the founding clan ancestor. The clan or '*par*' of any single village is often only one of many inhabiting a clan territory, the Pargana. At the level of Pargana, however all clans are related in a classificatory manner that is by an acknowledgement of common descent from an all embracing "ancestral deity" namely '*Barha Pen* (Popoff, 1980). There are two folds; one is the Pargana unit in which all clans are linked and the other is the village unit in which "*Barha Pen*" acts as either the progenitor or sibling of various specifically named ancestral deities. Therefore the stone is erected in their *katta* village. Here *katta* means clan village where their ancestral deity or founding clan ancestor is found. If a man dies in a village other than his natal village or if a women dies in a village other than her husband's natal village, or rather than natal village the tradition village of host his *katta,* then the stone is erected in the traditional *katta* village not in the village where he died. The Usendi woman died at Tondabera (Naghalpur) was buried at Tondabera but her marmangal (small cairn) was to be put up just outside the Usendi village of Orcha. Where, her husband's *katta* lives. The whole ceremony seems to be one of re-uniting the *hanals* with *bhum*, the earth and universal *hanal*, which they also say as their Bhera Pen (Hutton, 1931).

Elwin (1945) stated that the clan system of the Muria is very confused. In the olden days it seems probable that the inhabited territory of north Bastar was divided among the different clans of Muria and each had its own particular *bhum* or clan area. In each *bhum* there was a spiritual capital called the *pen-rawar* or *pen-kara*. Here lived the clan-god or *Anga* with the clan priest to tend him and mediate between him and his kinsmen. Here they came for the chief festivals of the *Anga* ; here they brought their dead and erected their menhirs..... there is one ancient *pen-rawar* to which the more orthodox elders of the tribe go when they can where they will have their menhirs erected. Beliefs in the clan *bhum* (Earth), whether original or adopted as a result of immigration and settlement is still sufficiently alive, to excite serious quarrels. It was a dispute over the rights to a clan bhum that began the deadly feud between the sorcerer Singlu and the people of Almer. Most of the inhabitants of Almer belong to the kaudo clan (which has its *pen-rawar* at kharkagaon) and they consider that the place is kaudo-bhum since they first settled there. But Singlu is a Karnaga. One day he said to the Kaudo priest; let me erect memorial stones in your village, and then my ancestors will live here and will help me and my family. But the priest pointed out that the headquarters of the Karnaga clan was at Kokori. If you bring your ancestors to this village, our gods will be neglected; he said and refused to give him any *bhum*.

The departed pot

In Bastar region the memorial practices is found on a traditional way, which highlights the importance of the dead to the outside world. But in the region the tribal society or family are giving more attention to the departed pot also known as *hanal kunda*.

Hill Maria: A large earthen pot is kept in inner room of a Hill Maria. Grigson described (1938) that in Hill Maria, the *lonu* room is essentially the room devoted to the departed *(hanal)* and is indeed, often referred to as the *hanal kholi* or "Room of the Departed". Here in a corner where rests the *hanal kunda* or pot of the departed, it is taboo for the husband to touch, and in which the housewife deposits a little meal for the departed ancestors. Whenever she grinds; and here is the *hanal oidal*, or the hearth of the departed, on which she cooks the first new grain at each of the new grain eating festivals; the ashes of this are never swept away. There is never a back door to the *lonu*. As no space should be wasted, there is always an *alpanji* platform in the *lonu* for storing provisions, specially jungle produce; but it is never slept on as women only may sleep in the *lonu,* and it is taboo for them to sleep anywhere except on the floor. At the funeral the Hill Marias sacrifice of cow and pig is generally performed in front of the pot of the departed.

Bison horn Maria: Earthen pot is kept in store room by the Bison horn Maria. The room where the pot in the name a deceased is kept is known as *wijja-lon*, which is used both as store room and for the cult of the departed. The third room of the home is used for this purpose. This room is generally used as the seed room or granary and is almost entirely filled with a large platform on which pots, baskets and snacks are placed. Bison horn Maria women cook new grain and various vegetables in the pot in the name of the departed at the *Kurum*, *Korta* and *Jata Pandum*. The husbands and other members of the family sacrifices chickens before the pot. The first solid food given to children is cooked in the pot at the Jata Pandum in December or January. In marriages the Perma of the village tells the head of the bridegrooms clan to cook in the Hanal-lon of the bride grooms house and when a bride comes to her new home, one of the things that the mother-in-law says to her is, "Now, this pot is yours".

Muria: The Muria also keep the pot in the name of deceased inside their houses, sometimes in the ordinary store-room and some often in the granary room. The departed pot is quite distinct from the little pots in which the soul of the dead man is believed to be brought back to the house and taken to the *Hanalkot* in order to be mingled with his house and clan ancestors. It is a permanent pot to which special offerings are made on all important occasions of Muria life. Women put a little rice and flour from time to time into the pot. Sometimes two pots were kept for the dead in the kitchen, one is filled of rice and the other is empty. During preparation of every meal the housewife transferred a pinch of rice to the empty pot in the honour of departed person. When the empty pot becomes full with rice, all the family members of the household cook and consume it. But the others not belong to the family clan. At an engagement ceremony, a cowrie is put in the pot to propitiate the family ancestors for the loss of girls from their clan. The clan dominates and controls the Muria social life. The Clan system retains its vitality both as exogamous unit and as a means of organizing its members round the Clan-god and the memory of the departed. Clan festivals remained great and notable occasions. Clan traditions still regulate funerary rites and memorial customs. There are various rules about this departed pot, only the married women and Gaita can remove and move towards the departed pot. When the newly bride comes home, it is the mothers responsibility to tell the above importance of the in the name of the deceased Pot. The Pot can be changed every year if the Pot is fractured due to any reasons.

Taboos related to Departed Pot

Elwin (1945), described various rules followed about this pot are "no man can remove anything form it. No unmarried girl above the age of puberty may approach it. The reason for this is that unmarried girls of the family will shortly be leaving the house and will be transferred to another clan and their connection will be with a different pot in someone else's house. At a Muria marriage also, when the bride comes to her new home, her mother-in-law shows her the pot of the Departed and rice -husker saying, "These things are now yours, care for us. Honour the dead, give food to all, entertain strangers".

Decoration of Memorials Pillars

The tribals of Bastar region decorate their house as they believe that they live in houses which are of their ancestors' house. They decorate the wooden fixtures of their houses and shrines with intricately carved upright poles, door panels, ceiling frames, etc. with carved motifs of birds, animals, human's figures, floral and geometric designs (Postel & Cooper, 1999). Accordingly they also carve their wooden memorial pillars. The use of similar kinds of motifs as in Indus Valley civilization proves that the craft had been existing from long, used by the villagers in their day to day livelihood (Elwin, 1951).

The wood carving in Bastar began in 13th century, when the artisans were scarce and the wood was easily available. Before 13th Century the tribes of the region used to do stone carving for erecting memorials. People started to meet their needs by carving out wood for erecting memorials and decoration purposes (Elwin, 1951). Gordon reported that at one time the Koruks erected stone memorial pillars of virgal type and that wooden memorials are derived from these, though it is possible that wooden and stone memorials at one time must have co-existed. This is the main theme of the memorial, but such symbols as jungle fowls, a spider and human ear, may be included.

Kamath, one of the historians who wrote in his book "*Memorials of the Middle East*", when the sculptors became scarce and sculpturing became expensive, people might have opted for carved wooden memorial. In Bastar where wood is abundant, they went in for the pillar type, whereas the eastern tribals preferred less expensive plank memorials. They used to erect carved memorials on the death of their relatives. This tradition came into supposed to be followed since Muria came into existence (Elwin, 1951). In Bastar, the Murias made small undistinguished pillars of wood in those areas where their megalithic cult has disappeared. The Kuruks of Indravati valley erected small pillars with the figure of bird cared on the top. It is only the Bison Horn Marias who have elaborated the practice.

Richard (1941) "*Indus Valley Painted Pottery*" has clearly illustrated and illuminatingly discussed many of the motifs which the tribesman using today on wall and door, on comb and tobacco case, the modern tribesman carve geometric symbolic design that are thousands of years old, going right back to the ancient civilization of Indus Valley. The basic motifs found in Indus Valley Civilization were very similar to Bastar motif such as triangle, swastika, meandering lines, animal, bird, fish, horn and bull head, sun, star, comb, plant, fish, bird, intersecting circle etc. He also said that during, Dussehra, one of the most famous festivals celebrated at the place, the tribesmen used to carve a Rath made of wood with just an axe, which carried by the king at the time in the procession. It was the Kakatiya dynasty, which provoked the artisan of Bastar to do it on larger scale and in making of monuments for their decoration purpose (as stated by the present king Kamal Chandra Bhanjdeo, Jagdalpur).

The decorations of the memorial pillars vary from area to area. The Maria of Chota Karkeli, Bara Karkeli, Kodepalli, Kutul etc. are erecting memorial pillar, which they look of as human body. The head of the memorial pillar is decorated with the wooden carving of cow/buffalo and Bison Horn Maria. But in Jagdalpur and Dantewada region the Bison horn Maria decorated upper portion of the memorial pillar with wooden carving elephant trunk, which carrying the symbols of wealth and power. There are common features in the memorial pillars of the region are the figurines of wooden pigeon are placed at the top.

The wooden or stone slab pillars are carved or painted the representation of ordinary objects and some interests of the dead man. Some of the scenes are chase of hunting in the forest, riding a horse, man carrying an earthen pot of *landa* (rice beer), agricultural activities life like planting seeds, ploughing and implements like axe, hoe etc.. Each memorial pillar in fact, attempts to be a biography in wood/ flat stone of the deceased. The lower portion of the memorial stone is supported with flat stone, sometimes they make mud platform. Every flat stone memorial pillars having notice board in their body, that indicated the name, birth and death date, village name, clan name and sometimes the causes of death. They also put cloths of departed in the memorial pillar. It has been observed in the Lohandiguda block that if they erect memorial of Siraha they put the traditional cloths on it, which seems to be a memorial pillar of Siraha.

Now in current scenario they are not erecting wooden memorials, generally they are using flat stone which are coated with white colour. The painter painted the biography of the deceased person with colourful paints available in local markets. Sometimes the flat stone is not coated with white colour, they just paint or simply write the name of the deceased person with black and yellow colours. Presently they are making concrete math with cement and bricks. Sometimes they make roof on it and generally painted with white colour.

The use of the local mythology and culture is easily noticeable in the memorials. They emphasized more on their local livelihood technique and use them again and geometric motif by hand gives somewhat more haphazard arrangements of themes. The motifs used in this craft mainly consist of the tribal life style and their livelihood. In the wooden memorial pillar the carving is done in the relief technique. The memorial pillars depicting tribal rituals and day to day life of tribal like that, Ghotul group dance, Bison Horn Maria Group dance, hunting scenes, agricultural activity scenes, and so on.

Importance of Megalithic practices

The importance of megalithic tradition in the region leads the harmony in their culture. The people of this region who erect memorials are controlled by the rule of clan endogamy. Every village has its clan territory, and the memorials are erected in these territories. No one can erect their memorials in others clan territory. These memorials are treasured, honoured and worshipped by the community concerned. Some of the importance, of erecting memorials are as follows:-

i. Generally the memorials are sign of respect, love of tributes for their departed family members.

ii. Memorial pillars are the gateway between the world of man and paradisean world. After death the soul goes to Mahaprabhu, and one lived in the departed pot, lives in the house as a god (deo). In several occasions they are worshipped. There is a belief that the memorial stones grow in size if the spirit of the dead is satisfied with the arrangements that are made for him. Late Singlu of Lalsunar village (2015) told that he has seen the feeble growth of stones in size. When a stone grows it is considered fortunate. There is sure to be happiness and good luck for the family concerned. If a stone falls dons or goes bent, the relatives consult the Siraha and then put it straight and offer whatever sacrifices he recommends. It is generally supposed that when a stone falls, it is an indication that the ghost of the dead is angry or feels neglected.

iii. It has been reported that Hill Marias of Abujmarh erects their memorials on slope hills and forest sometimes in their agricultural fields. It is believed that ancestor protect their hill, forest and agricultural fields from evil and unnatural events.

iv. There is a belief that, if they erect memorials and worship them they earn blessings of their ancestors which helps to lead health and prosperous life.

v. Every clan groups are maintaining their memorials separately as erected in their own clan territory. The memorials are not only for showcasing but it also indicate that their living members of a particular clan group belong to this territory (*bhum*), and all common resources having the rights over it.

vi. The customs and practices of memorials of the region, showing the respect of the person after death. This helps to maintain peace, unity, brotherhood, and preservation of their rich cultural tradition. Various types of motifs carved in the memorial pillars reflect the relationship between the indigenous ecology and the tribals.

vii. The Memorials help to recall their predecessors in chronological order and numbers.

viii. The living megalithic practices are still in the form of traditional way. But it has also witnessed the changes in their memorials. The adjustment between old and new tradition in their memorials are sustaining in their day to day life. It can be reported seeing the motifs that, the modern amenities like cycle, umbrella, motor cycle, television, mobile etc. are important component in their life. Similarly these are the current objects which are drawn in their memorial pillars. Even the motif of aero plan on memorials and aero plan shape *maths* are substituted in the areas.

ix. The practice of megalithic tradition in Bastar region is to be set up in the memory of deceased persons not only for their future fame. It is their own and local prestige of their kin members who bear the expenses. During the rituals of erecting memorials, all the clan members (both *akomama* and *dadabhai*) gather in their *bhum* (Earth) and each and every family share their expanses. Which shows that, how a society helps to build a strong bond to each other's, collective strength of the clan group, sharing attitude among the clan members.

7

CHAPTER

A PICTORIAL VIEW OF MEMORIALS IN THE HONOUR OF DEAD'S IN BASTAR

The megalithic cultures reached in India form east and west, the former in Neolithic age and the latter in the early Iron Age. There is a close connection in their process of megalithic culture, in the Gonds of Bastar, the Hill tribes of Orissa and Chotanagpur, the Nagas and the Khasi of North Eastern State. In Central India mainly in Bastar region (*Old Bastar dynasty*) the customs of erecting memorial pillars is prevalent in large scale among different tribal groups. Some of the groups are Bison Horn Maria, Hill Maria, Muria, Raj Gonds etc.

Figure: 1: *Ethnography Map of Bastar (Old Bastar dynasty)*

Source: Anthropological Survey of India, Jagdalpur

Some of the Lists of major sites of memorials in Bastar region

Area/ District	Name of the Scheduled Tribes	Locality of Memorial Sites	Type of memorials covered during filed work
Bastar	Bison Horn Maria	Kodenar, Arma Para	Printed memorial pillar, Math, Wooden Madia Khambha
		Palnar/ Palanar	Printed memorial pillar and Stone (Kal) memorial Pillar
		Khilepal, Patel Para	Printed memorial pillar and Math
		Bastanar, Nakapara,	Printed memorial pillar, Math, Wooden Madia Khambha.
		Bastanar, Erpa	Uraskal, Madia Khamba, and Math
		Bastanar, Bara Bodenar, Sadra Bodenar	Uraskal, Madia Khamba, Biti, Stone memorial pillar and Math
		Bastanar, Patel Para, Kolia Para	Uraskal, Madia Khamba, Biti, Stone memorial pillar and Math
		Kurushpal, Bastar	Math and Stone memorial pillar
		Jamgaon, Bastanar	Painted memorial pillar
		Tumpani Bastar	Math and Stone memorial pillar
		Matenar	Math and Madia Khamba
		Michnar	Math and wooden Pillars (*Madia Khambha*)

Dantewada	Bison Horn Maria	Poyami para of Metanar (Poyami para	Uraskal
		Netapur (Patel para)	Uraskal
		Faraspal, Dantewada	Uraskal, Math, Stone memorials
		Alnar, Dantewada	Uraskal, Stone memorial pillars
		Dhurli, Dantewada	Uraskal (site is protected by Archaeological Survey of India)
		Gamawada	Uraskal (this site is also protected by Archaeological Survey of India)
Bijapur	Bison Horn Maria	Kuturu	Stone memorials with Gour head.
		Karkeli (Bara & Chotta Karkeli), Bhairamgarh (Bijapur)	Stone memorials with Gour head.
Narayanpur	Muria	Binjhil, Narayanpur	Kal Khunta
		Dev Gaon, Narayanpur	Kal Khunta and Gata Khunta
		Lalsunhar, Narayanpur	Kal Khunta
		Sulenga, Narayanpur	Kal Khunta
	Abhujmaria	Kurushnar, Narayanpur	Stone Memorial
		Orcha, Narayanpur	Stone Memorial

The tribal groups believed that if the dead soul is satisfied with the arrangements of Kin groups, the stone grows. The soul of the deceased stays in the stone. When the family gets a new born child, the soul will come with. The departed soul also protects the deceased family from devil. The maximum period of worshipping the stone is twenty -forty years.

The first documentation of Megalithic culture in Chhattisgarh is by J.D. Begler in Report on tour in Central Provinces (ASI Report 1878), where he has given information about groups of Menhirs, Cairns Circles in 1873 during his archaeological tour to Chhattisgarh. The architectural designs of the memorial structures found in different places in Bastar are varied from each other. As the Stone Age legacy, dating back to the Iron Age passed on to the successive generations, the tribals of Bastar have continued this tradition. The tradition, according to anthropologist has come to Bastar from the Indonesian archipelago and to the north-eastern region of India and Orissa through Burma (Vinay, 2018).

Figure: 2: *Muria couple*

Figure: 3: *Muria Women during the rituals*

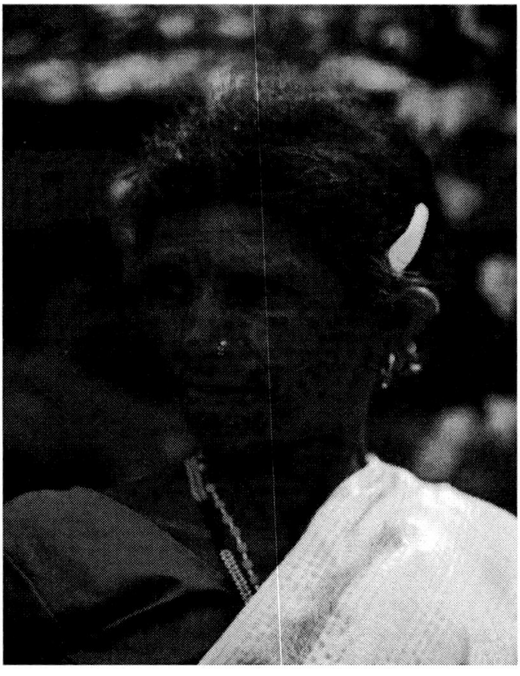

Figure: 4: *Hill Maria (Abhujmaria) Women*

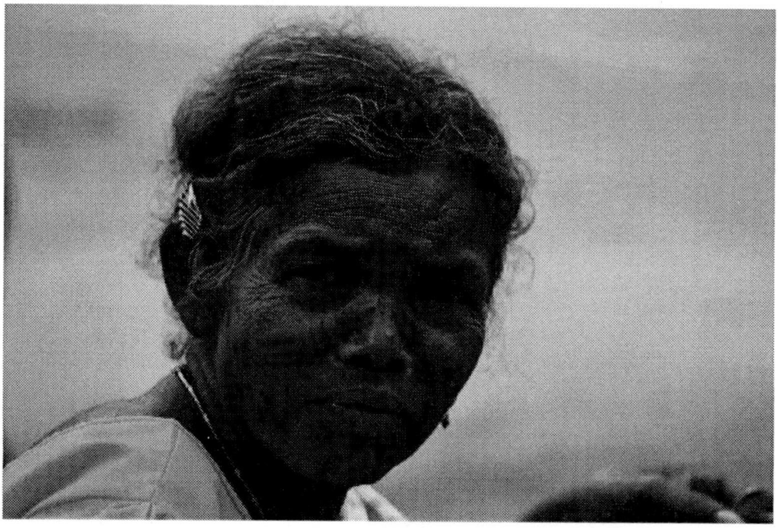

Figure: 5: *Hill Maria (Abhujmaria) Women*

Figure: 6: *Anga Deo (Deity)*

Figure: 7: *Muria with Anga Deo (Deity)*

According to Elwin (1947), the Anga is in form and character unique among the aboriginal gods of India. In form it is an arrangement of three parallel poles...... over which are tied.... Cross pieces of bamboo or Saja. The central pole is the actual god, the two sides –poles being simply intended to enable his two or four bearers to raise him and carry him about.

Figure: 8: *Muria couple with traditional attire*

Figure: 9: *Dandami Maria (Bison Horn Maria) women with their traditional ornaments*

Figure: 10: *Musical Instrument-Dhol (Mandri)*

Figure: 11: *Muria Men with Dhol (Mandri)*

Playing with drums, moves in a large circle with a great variety of turns and changes.

Figure: 12: *Hunting Horn (Thodi)*

The Ghasi community makes an elaborate brass horn by the cire-perduce process. Hunting horn are blown at festivals to announce the arrival of a god or to mark any important turn of the ceremonial.

A. Types of Memorial Pillars found in Bastar region

Figure: 13: *Uraskal (menhir) in Gammawada, Dantewada district.*

Figure: 14: *Uraskal (menhir) in Gammawada, Dantewada district.*

Figure: 15: *Painted memorial Pillar, Bade Kilepal, Bastar District.*

One of the important sites found in Gammawada, village in the district Dantewada. It is 100 kilometre from Jagdalpur city. It is situated in the Jagdalpur –kirnadul highway. Thousands of thousand *uraskal* (menhir) are erected here. It has been reported that the site is more than two thousand year old. The row of uraskal at Gammawada represents an individual member of the family. Gammawada is the clan village, and it has its own territory. The clan members of Gammawada village are scattered in nearby villages namely Farashpal, Patras, Kumahras, Bhasi, Kameli, Bacheli, Dhurli, Nerli, Chandenar etc.. Every year they all gathered in their clan village to celebrated *Marka Pandum, Mati Tihar* and *Navakhai.* It has been discussed in the previous chapter that "as a rule memorials are erected within the territory (bhum) of a clan, though active participation in the rituals of an ancestral village". Both the above sites are currently under the protection of Archaeological Survey of India (Figure- 1 & 2).

The painted memorial pillar is situated in Bade Kilepal very near to road side. The brightly painted memorial is in the name of Sunderlal Poyam, age-30 years, village-Bade Kilepal and death of year is 2007. If you see the memorial it has been clearly understood that the deceased person was departed due to a motorcycle accident. The memorial pillar was reported in the year 2015, and the said memorial was erected in 2007 (Figure-3).

Figure: 16: *Painted memorial Pillar, Jamgaon (Bastanar), Bastar District.*

Two brightly painted memorial pillars are located in village Jamgaon, Bastanar tehsil of Bastar district. It is situated two km away from sub-district headquarter Bade Kilepal and 59 km away from district headquarter, Jagdalpur.

If we see the picture which has been painted in the pillars are a mixture of both their traditional life and modern. The upper portions of the pillars are decorated with wood, which mark out with head of cows.

The middle portion of the pillars depicts their traditional way of life. The women with their dancing stick, male dancer, pots of beer, large drums are typical of these areas. It is believe that dancing and liquor are pleasures that the departed enjoyed when he was alive.

Figure: 17: *Painted memorial pillar near Gammawada, Dantewada district.*

A painted memorial pillar is situated near to Gammawada, Dantewada. The pillar is erected on the platform made by cement and concrete. The upper and middle portion of the pillars is a flat stone (in the region sedimentary rock is found frequently), painted with white background.

The motif of the pillar is painted with modern touch. mobile with charger, water glass, vanity bag, etc., and a picture of deceased women are painted.

Figure 18: *Stone memorial pillars with wooden replicas of buffalo horns and birds, Kutru, Bijapur district.*

These types of memorial are erected in Kutru, Bijapur region by Bison horn Maria. There is an upright flat stone and a replica of buffalo's horn and two pigeons (bird) are decorated in the top of the memorial.

Figure: 19: *Stone memorial pillars with wooden replicas of buffalo horns and birds, in Village Museli, near Kutru, Bijapur district.*

The memorial pillar erected in the village Museli, Kutru, Bijapur. These memorials are made of both stone and wood. The main features of these memorials are replicas of wooden buffalo horns (Figure- 5 & 6).

Figure: 20: *Carved wooden memorial Pillar, near Pakhnar, Jagdalpur.*

The picture shows the wooden pillar, generally erected by the Bison horn Maria of Bastar. This eight feet wooden pillar is square in shape. The pillar is made of Saja (*Terminalia Tomentosa*) wood. The wooden pillar is divided into five portions, first upper portion have two domes. The second portion is a man (mainly the deceased person) himself riding on an elephant with an umbrella and an axe along with bag hanging in shoulder. On the third portions, there is a picture of agricultural activities like weeding grass in the crop field by women, ploughing the crop field with bullock etc., the forth portion is all about the man dancing with their Bison horn Maria head-dresses along with *dhol* and girls dancing with their dancing sticks, which is the last portion of the wooden pillar.

This wooden pillar is situated in Pakhnar, Jagdalpur. When a well-known and wealthy man dies, his family erects a carved wooden pillar to his memory. The wooden pillar is more expensive, therefore who have economically sound the family member erects carved wooden pillar in the memory of departed person. These pillars are called by Grigson '*urasgatta,* a word that is obviously formed on the same plan as *uraskal* from *urasana* meaning to bury and *gatta*- 'a pillar'.

In front of the wooden pillar a small cromlech (pieces of small stone slab) is made at the bottom or front of the pillar. This is known as ghost's throne, which is set up by *Akomamas* or wife clan members. This cromlech is used for offering chicken, grain, liquor etc. to the departed person (Figure-7).

Such pillars attempt to be a biography in wood of the deceased.

Figure: 21: *Wooden Pillar (Plain) near Bade Kilepal, Bastar district.*

This wooden pillar from the roadside of Bade kilepal, first pillar is in slender shape and other is in square. Both the pillars having small cromlech and length of the pillars are about four feet long.

Figure: 22: *Stone Memorial Pillar with wooden top, Pakhnar, Bastar District.*

These types of stone memorials (*uraskal*) are found everywhere in the Jagdalpur area. Bison horn Maria continues to erect for their men, women and children.

This stone memorial is situated near Pakhnar village. The size of the erected stone is four feet long and almost two feet broad (Figure-9).

The cremation ground is always on the road side of the path or road, opposite to the row of menhir erected to honour the dead. In front of the memorial stone there is a small stone which is known as throne of departed. Some areas it has been known as ghost's throne. Sister's son play leading role touches the stone and addressed the dead man and says "this is selected for you, live with happily". Then stone is carried to the place where it is to be erected (Figure- 8 & 9).

***Figure:* 23:** *Stone Memorial Pillar, Bastanar, Jagdalpur.*

The erected memorial is located in Bastanar, Jagdalpur. This is one of the biggest memorial pillars (thirteen feet long) in the area in a road side. Both the road side there are several small and big size memorial pillars. The selected stone is carried with the help of kin members where the hole is dug by the sister's son, relatives and other members. Before the stone is erected the *Gaita* addresses the dead, 'you are dead and you must forget your father, your mother, your brother and your family, this is your house, live here and does not trouble ours or ours pigs and cattle. We are giving you rice and pulses and everything that you had at home, so that you may be satisfied'.

Figure: 24: *Bitti (mounds of stone) in addition to the rows of uraskal.*

Some Bison horn Maria honour their dead with *biti* in addition to the rows of *uraskal*. There are small/large heaps of stones, each surmounted by an upright stone. Each *biti* commemorates a single individual. Relatives and kin members of the deceased contribute stones during the building of the memorial such structure. Now days the practice of raising such mounds of stone has been discontinued by the Bison horn Maria.

Figure: 25: *Math (Cenotaphs) near Faraspal village, Dantewada district.*

This type of *Math* (Cenotaphs) is common seen on the road side of Dantewada to Barsur road or in Jagdalpur to Chitrakote road. This maths are made of bricks, stones and cements and painted with white colour.

It has been reported that this is the easiest way to erect memorials for departed. Now days it has been difficult to obtain big stones or suitable wood used for erecting. We can say that this is the substitutes of menhir.

Figure: 26: *Math (Cenotaphs) at Kutru, Bijapur district.*

This is the example of ancient custom with modern innovations. This math is situated in the dense forest of Kutru area.

These two *maths*, are related to the Kunjam family. It seems that the people here that is in Kutru that comes from the backward area of Bijapur district, are also brining changes in the process of building their memorials to their deceased person.

B. Process of erecting Memorials

Figure: 27: *Clan members arrived in village for the rituals.*

Figure: 28: *Clan members arrived in village along with necessary commodities.*

As soon as the family members of the departed person gathered enough money and grains needed in the process of erecting menhir He messages all his relatives (both *dadabhai* and *akomama*) and neighbours to gather in a fixed date. Accordingly, both dadabhia and akomama reaches the village where the menhirs are erected along with inviting's provisions such as grain, salt, *landa*, mahua liquor, pulses, new cloths (dhoti, saree etc.) etc. along with that, they also bring goat, cow, buffalo and pig with them.

Figure: 29: *Traditional way of welcoming their family members/ clan member/saga etc.*

A group of female members welcomes the kin members. In this process, they clean the feet with water and give an Arti to them with their traditional Diya (lamp). After this they apply hinges in their forehead and face. Hinges is made of a mixture of oil, rice and turmeric (Figure- 28 & 29).

Figure: 30: *Traditional way of welcoming their family members/ clan member/saga etc.*

Women welcome their *saga*/kin members, who came to participate in the functions with respect and thank them.

Figure: 31: *Woman folk gathered from different villages for erecting uraskal, in the name of departed.*

In 2014, a ceremony called *Gata Pakhna* (*uraskal*) was done in Sulenga village, Narayanpur. Where 35 departed persons family are gathered for erecting *uraskal* in the honour/memory of their deceased in past 20 years. All the deceased people are belong to *Gaita* and *Mata Pujari* family.

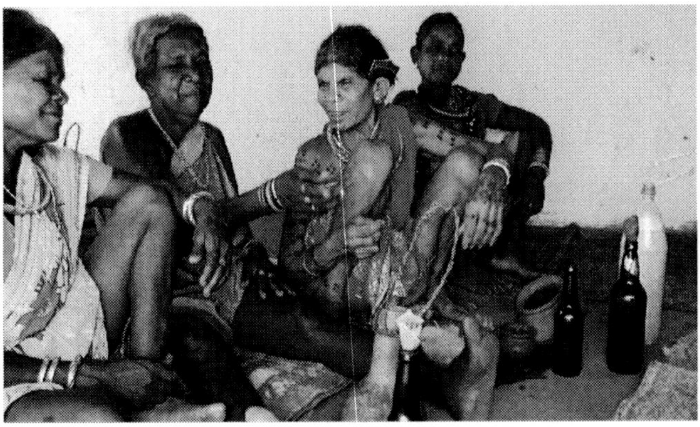

Figure: 32: *Pat Dokri who sings Hanal Pata Song.*

Group of elderly women invited for singing *Hanal Pata* Song (death/burial songs), during the *Gata Khunta* Ceremony. They are locally known as *Pat Dokri*. Only women are entitled to do so.

Figure: 33: *Pat Dokri along with their assistant.*

Pat Dokari accompanied by her assistant known as *Rocheg* in Gondi language. The main motive of the songs are not merely remembered the dead, but are welcome with affection and respect to unite with their ancestors. The names of the departed were mentioned during singing and it is a continuously process. During the verse each departed are requested to visit *Kalarpara* (where mahua liquor are distilled and sold), and mock Bazaar (*Hatum*). Figure: 33- A Group of *Pata Dokra* (a group of male members who sang Pata during rituals)

Figure: 34: *A Group of Pata Dokra (a group of male members who sang Pata during rituals)*

Figure: 35: *Akomama prepares cooked food for offering*

Akomama preparing cooked food for offering to the departed during the ceremony of gata khunta. The clan members which they can marry are Akomamas.

Figure:36: *Selection of stone for departed person*

A view of gathering for selection of stone in the name of departed person. Siraha, who identify the each stone for the family concerned for the erection of *uraskal* (stone memorial pillar).

Figure: 37: *Akomama carrying the selected stone for erection.*

Akomama, who is the sole responsible for carrying the stone in his shoulder, and erection of *uraskal*

Figure: 38: *Akomama's carrying the selected stone for erection.*

Akomama, carrying the stone, wrapped with white cotton cloths, where the erection process is done.

Figure: 39: *A view of Bazaar ceremony (Hatum).*

A view of Bazaar ceremony (*hatum*), at this time the souls of dead are supposed to mingle with their own ancestors. The activities of the Bazar were carried out in a light hearted manner and everyone participated in the revelry.

Figure: 40: *A view of Bazaar ceremony (hatum).*

Figure: 41: *Last offerings to the Earth (Bhum).*

Last offerings to the Earth (*Bhum*) in the name deceased person in Bazaar ceremony (*hatum*) for well-being of future generation and desire to bring happiness and good luck to the family concerned.

Figure: 42: *Involving in the process of their ancestors in a proper place with dance and music.*

Figure: 43: *Family members express their gratitude to Akomamas.*

For his jobs and responsibility (*Akomama*), family members express their gratitude that he came and do all the ceremonies on behalf of their family. So in the last day of the *gata khunta* Ceremony they roll around on their shoulder in *hatum* (Bazar Ceremony). It can be seen as a farewell ceremony.

Figure: 44

Figure: 44

Protection of these wooden memorial pillars is necessary for preservation of these age old tradtion (Figure 43 & 44) which is still prevalent in the tribal societ of Bastar.

8

CHAPTER

CONCLUSION

Megalithic practices having close link with burial sites, most of them were erected during Neolithic period. The age old tradition of megalithic practices is still continuing in Bastar region. In the process of cultural assimilation they have lost some of their traditional way of life as well as they have also adopted the culture of non-tribal living around them. In the era of 21st century, they have been maintaining the erection of Memorial Pillars in the name of departed soul. The traditions of erecting memorials are practicing throughout the India. Form the Sabars of West Bengal, Mundas and Oraons of Odisha to Nagas of the North East, worshiping the dead to ensure rebirth and also blessing from the departed soul. In this regard, the erecting process and tradition of Muria, Maria and Hill Maria of the Bastar region are also as same from the others. They erect megaliths in memory of the dead, confirming their beliefs in the existence of soul after death. They believe that there is a life after death, human has two souls, the life sprit and the shadow. The shadow must be prevented from returning to its home, or it will harm the surviving relatives. The life spirit goes to *mahaprabhu* (God). The shadow stays in the family after the erection of a memorial pillar. These ancestor spirits watch over the moral manners of the living and punish offender of traditional law. The erecting of memorial pillars in the memorial of the departed is still persisting among the aborigines, which depict their traditional way of life and their grave art.

In the context of tribal Bastar, when a person deceases the concerned family observes seven to fifteen days mourning period as per custom. After mourning for six months to one year they observed different types of ancestral ceremonies. But in case of Muria, Maria and Hill Maria they do erect memorials in the name of departed person. The process of erecting memorials is varying from each other and slightly varies from area to area. These are *Kal Khunta, Gata Pakhna, Gata Khunta, Madia Khambha* etc. which have same objectivity. Different types of memorial pillars erected in Bastar region are *danyakal, urasgutta* (wooden pillar), *uraskal* (stone memorial), Painted Memorial, Math (cenotaph) etc. Elwin in his paper "Funerary customs in Bastar State, 1945" reported that two types of megalithic monuments are erected. The dead are prone to take offence, suspicious, extremely revengeful and unsympathetic; the living aborigine left no stone unturned to keep them in their place. So that the dead could find some warmth and love and receive the comfort they needed. Similarly, Hutton concurs that a memorial affords a temporary dwelling for the soul "pending its operation as a fertilizer of the crop". It is an ancient belief that while a tribal leads a life in his own desired space he or she is given some space even after the death and lives at that place as living soul and the spirits of wealthy men are endowed with the magical power to enhance the good fortunes of a community.

Different etymology of Memorials: In Elwins words "to have carved pillar in your memory is the Maria equivalent of being buried in Westminster abbey". Grigson identifies the wooden pillar - the term *urasgatta* (derived from *urasana* meaning -'to bury' and *gatta*-'a pillar'). The Maria calls the pillar either *munde* or madia *kambha*.

Expensiveness and time duration: The ceremony of erecting memorials are very expensive, therefore the families are forces to postpone it to a future. When sufficient provisions are collected in the home they desired to this last rites. It has been reported that some families in the study area erect their memorial pillars for their ancestor after the death of 30 years.

Impact of modernization on Memorial Pillars: The concept of Megalithic practices has changed which can be observed that previously they erect crude and rough Memorial pillars now days they are prepared cemented cenotaphs and the painted memorials. But the basic concept of megalithic practices remains unchanged in the region. The rich and influential people in the society or who hold some powerful position, as Patel, village headman, politician, etc. have losing the essence of crude and rough memorials. Apart from this, large numbers of tribal are migrating from rural to urban area, which resulted in the form of various modern touched memorial pillars. There are many other problems that obstruct the practice of this age old tradition. The one of the major problem is expenditure of the feast which has to be borne at the time of the erection of the memorials by the deceased relatives and family members.

Protection of Memorial Pillars: The protections of Memorial Pillars are necessary and somewhat the local administrations are also doing. The wooden memorials cannot stand the ravage of the weather, termite and fungal attack. In the area all the wooden memorial pillars not in a good condition, most of them do not last more than a decade. They are dismissing very fastly. Nowadays, the stone pillars at Gamawada and wooden memorial pillars at Dilmili have been protected monuments under the Ancient monuments and archaeological sites remains Acts 1958.

There are many sites scattered in the area, but few of them has been protected.

Elwin has made it very clear that the Gonds of Bastar imagine the departed as capable of both beneficial and harmful intervention in human affairs and this belief in the unity of the dead and the living is indeed one of the cardinal features of megalithic religion. The memorial ceremonies are obligatory in their life as it has been reported in the Binjhi village of Narayanpur district, eight families had migrated to Maharashtra in the year 1970s but in 2001 they came back to their village for erection of memorials for their ancestors. Therefore in the tribal societies who are associated with memorials pillars are survival and not only perpetuation of the clan but also present a brief clan detail about their ancestors through this pillar to their future generation *uraskal, danyakal, kal khunta, madia khambha,* painted stone pillar etc. not only represents the last stages of life but also promote spiritual union with ancestors, in honour of the dead. That's why each stone, wooden pillar adds to the collective power of the monastic group as a whole and ultimately the clan that is associated with the earth and the spirits of the departed. Now days it would be truthful to say that impact of modernization, migration/rural exodus, degradation of the environment, industrialization etc. is also seen in the practices of memorial monuments. For all these reasons, the adequate measures must be developed to safeguard this heritage.

BIBLIOGRAPHY

Agarwal, P.C. (1968). Human Geography of Bastar District. Allahabad. Ganga Brothers.

Alekshin, V, A. (1983). Burial Custom as an Archaeological source. Current Anthropology, Vol. 24. No. 2, The University of Chicago Press, Wenner - Gren Foundation for Anthropological Research.

Binford, L. R. (1971). Mortuary practices: Their study and their Potential, In Approaches to the Social Dimension of Mortuary Practices. Washington DC, Memoirs of the Society for American Archaeology, No. 25.

Childe, V. Gordon. (1948). Megaliths, Ancient India: Number - 4, Bulletin of the Archaeological Survey of India (July 1947-1948). New Delhi, Archaeological survey of India.

Cooper, Z. (1997). Prehistory of the Chitrakot Falls, Central India. Pune, Ravish Publishers.

De Breet, H. (1909). Chhattisgarh and Feudatory States Gazetteer: The Bastar and Kanker states from the present District of Bastar, Bombay, Central Provinces Gazetters.

Elwin, Varrier, (1943). The Maria Murder and Suicide. London, Oxford University Press.

------------------- (1945). Funerary customs in Bastar State. Man in India.

------------------(1950). Bondo highlander. London, Oxford University Press.

------------------(1947). The Muria and their Ghotul. Bombay, Oxford University Press.

---------------------(1964). The Tribal World of Varrier Elwin, Bombay, Oxford University Press.

Glasfurd, C. L.R. (1863). Report on the Dependency of Bastar. Calcutta. Selection from records of the Government of India, Foreign Department, No. XXXIX

Grigson, Sir. Wilferd. (1938). The Maria Gonds of Bastar. London, Oxford University Press.

Gupta, Chandrasekhar. ed. by R.K. Sharma. (1982). Megalithic Culture of Dakshina Kosal, (Indian Archaeology New Perspective

Gurdon, P.R.T, (1907). The Khasis, London. Macmillan & Co. Ltd.

Hajra, D. (1970). The Dorla of Bastar, Memoir no. 17, Calcutta, Anthropological Survey of India.

Haimendorf, F. V. C. (1943). Megalithic Rituals among the Gadabas and Bondos of Orissa. Journal of Royal Asiatic Society Bengal.

Haimendorf, F. V. C. (1945). The Problem of Megalithic Cultures in Middle India. Man in India 25(2)

Hutton, J.H, (1935). Census of India, Vol. I, Part-III, Ethnographical, Government India Press.

Hutton, J.H, (1922). The Meaning and Method of the Erection of Monoliths by the Naga Tribes, The Journal of the Royal Anthropological Institute of Great Britain and Ireland, Vol. 52 (June-Dec, 1922).

Hodson, T.C. (1937). India. Census Ethnography 1901-1931, published by the Manager of Publication, Government of India Press, New Delhi.

Huber, W. A. (1975). From Millennia to Millennium: An Anthropological History of Bastar State, a thesis is submitted in University of British Columbia, Faculty of Graduate Study (Dept. of Anthropology and Sociology)

Jagathpathi, G. (1964). Census of India, 1961, Madhya Pradesh, District Census Handbook, Bastar District, Government of Madhya Pradesh.

Kaufmann, Walter. (1960). The Songs of the Hill Maria, Jhoria Maria and Bastar Muria Gond Tribes, Ethnomusicology, Vol. 4, No. 3(Sep. 1960), University of Illinois Press.

Kedarnath, P. (1937). Bastar Bhushan: Hindi History of Bastar Estate, Benares.

Mazumdar, D.N, (ed). (1962). Caste and Communication in an Indian village. Asia publication house, Bombay.

Malinowaski, B. (1948). Magic, Science and Religion and Other Eassays, The Free Press, Glencoe Illinois, USA.

Moorti U.S (1994). Megalithic Culture of South India: Socio-Economic Perspectives, Ganga Kaveri Publication, Varanasi.

Popoff, Terrel. (1980). The Muriya and Tallur Mutte: A Study of the Concept of the Earth Among the Muriya Gonds of Bastar District, India. Unpublished Doctoral Dissertation, University of Sussex.

Moorti, U.S., 1994 Megalithic Culture of South India, A Socio-Economic Perspective, Ganga Kaveri Publication, Varanasi

Moorti, U.S., 1994 Megalithic Culture of South India, A Socio-Economic Perspective, Ganga Kaveri Publication, Varanasi

Moorti, U.S., 1994 Megalithic Culture of South India, A Socio-Economic Perspective, Ganga Kaveri Publication, Varanasi

Poster, M. & Copper, Z. (1999). Bastar Folk Art: Shrines, Figures and Memorials, Franco Indian Research Private Limited, Mumbai.

Rao, S. N. (1991). Megalithic practice among the Khasis and Nagas of North Eastern India In: Singh, J P and Sengupta, G eds. Archaeology of North Eastern India. New Delhi: Har Anand Publications – Vikas Publishing House Pvt. Ltd.

Ravdonikas, V. I. (1932). The Cave Cities of the Crimea and the Problem of the Goths in Connection with the Stage. By Stage Development of the Northern Black Sea Coastal Region (in Russian). Izveshiya Gosudrstvenoni Akademii Materialnoi Kultury.

Richard, Starr. F. S. (1941). Indus Valley Painted Pottery: A Comparative study of the Design on the Painted Wares of the Harappa Culture. Princeton, Princeton University Press.

Russel, R. V. & Hiralal R. B. (1916). Tribes and Castes of Central Provinces of India. Vol. III. London. Macmillan & Co. Ltd.

Singh, K.S. (ed). (1993). Tribal Ethnography, Customary Law and Change: New Delhi: Concept Publishing Company.

Singh, U. (2016). A History of Ancient and Early Medieval India: From the Stone Age to the 12th Century. Noida, Uttar Pradesh, Pearson India Education Services Pvt. Ltd.

Sharma, A.K. (2000). Archaeo - Anthropology of Chhattisgarh. New Delhi, Sandeep Prakashan.

Temple, R. (1923). Report on the administration of the Central Provinces up to August 1862, Nagpur.

Thakur, K. P. (1908). Bastar Bushan (Hindi History of Bastar) Benares, Bharat Jiwan Press.

Thusu, K. P. (1965). The Dhurwa of Bastar. Memoir no. 16, Calcutta. Anthropological Survey of India.

Troisi. J. (2000). Tribal Religion: Religious Beliefs and Practices among the Santals. New Delhi.

Yidyarthi L.P. (1961). Sacred Complex of Hindu Gaya, Bombay Asia Publishing House.

Vinay, K. (2018). Rituals and Practices Associated with the Megaliths of Bastar. Journal of Multidisciplinary studies in Archaeology 6.

GLOSSARY

Koitor	A Gondi term denoting themselves as koitor
Dippa/Penda	Slash and Burn Cultivation/Hoe Cultivation
Gotra	Clan
Kosra	A type of rice
Kutki	A type of Millet (Panicum Miliaceum)
Dadabhai	Brothers clan members
Akkomama	Wife's clan members
Katta	Known as totemistic clan
Pen	God
Mur	Palash tree
Deogudi	Known as sacred place found in every village in Bastar region
Pedda	Head of traditional political system in Bison Horn Maria. The Post is hereditary
Pujari/Gaita/Waddai/ Gunia	Sacred Specialist
Dungri	Mountain or High place
Hanal Pata	Burial song in Gondi dialect
Khambhas/Stambhas	Memorial pillar/Post
Bhum	Earth
Anga Dev	Village deity

Uraskal	Menhir
Dhanyakal	Dolmen/Cap Stone
Urasgutta	Wooden/Stone memorial Pillar/post
Pathri	Stone Circle
Marghat	Burial Ground
Vadki Kal	Process of meeting
Mand	Liquor
Chind	Date Palm (Phoenix Canariensis)
Mandari	Drum (dhol)
Todi	Hunting Horn
Dapa	Different types of leave plates
Gato Dapa	Used for rice serving
Pula Dapa	Used for vegetables serving
Java Dapa	Used for Pej (Gruel made of husk rice) drinking
Hatum	Mock Bazar
Alignment	A series of menhirs arranged in lines on some definite system
Avenue	Two or more aligments approximately parallel with one another
Megalithic	Made of large stone (From the Greek: megas- great, and lithos- Stone)
Cromelch	Post of small stone also known as Cyclolith.
Menhir	Simplest of all the megalithic monuments, consisting of a single monolith set up, as a rule at or near a burial spot. The monolith may be small or gigantic in height with its base fixed into the earth. In Bastar State, it is known as uraskal (Gondi: urasna- to bury and Dravadian: Kal- stone) and ususally occurs there in an alignment of menhirs

Cairn	A Cairn is a barrow made of heaped-up stone rubble
Dolmen	(Celtic: dol, table and men-stone) A single slab of stone supported by several orthostatic boulders or slabs build on the surface of the ground in such a way as to enclose a space or chamber beneath the capstone. It may or may not be with or without a port hole known in Bastar State where it is placed at the bottom of the memorial pillar as hanal gharia (ghost –throne) also known as danyakal.
Small Bamboo Basket	Gappa
Kochai Kanda	Colocasia Tubers
Flat Bread	Akki/Chila made of rice flour
Dhusir	Paddy wrapped in straw
Saga	Kin/Clan Members
Pitre	Memorial feast
Gariyakal	A Upper Stone
Hanagunda	Clan Priest, each and every Clan has its own Hanagunda
Jiwa/Jiva	Soul
Hanal	Association of the dead
Rawr	Temple
Gutta	Wooden Post
Suta	Iron ring for neck
Hanal Kutul	Ghost Stool
Kotokal	As the place where the memorial are located
Iron Ring	Wadkia (Finger ring)
Saja Tree	Terminalia Tomentosa
Aden Tree	Alstonia Venenatus

Bird	Pite
Bhandari Ghar	Temporary shelter of leaves of wild date Plam
Chhind	Wild date Palm
Gutta	Post
Koda	Horse
Erramtogh	Senior wife Clan relative
Landa	Rice-beer
Small Cairn	Marma Kal/Marman Gal